D0542814

PHAEDRA BRITANNICA

Other works by
Tony Harrison

Earthworks 1964
Aikin Mata (with James Simmons) 1966
Newcastle is Peru 1969
The Loiners 1970
The Misanthrope 1973
Palladas: Poems 1975

PHAEDRA

BRITANNICA

by Tony Harrison
after Jean Racine

LONDON
REX COLLINGS

First published by Rex Collings Ltd
69 Marylebone High Street, London W1

Reprinted 1975
Second Edition 1975
Third edition (with introductory essay
& illustrations) 1976

Paper SBN 901720 75 5
Cloth ISBN 086 036019 9

All applications to perform this play
should be made to Fraser & Dunlop (Scripts) Ltd
91 Regent Street, London W1

Typesetting by Malvern Typesetting Services Ltd,
Printed in Great Britain at the
University Printing House, Cambridge
(Euan Phillips, University Printer)

PREFACE

Prétends-tu m'éblouir des Fables de la Grèce? . . .
Quoiqu'au-dessus de nous ils sont ce que nous somnes,
Et comme nous enfin les Héros sont des Hommes.
Pradon *Phèdre et Hippolyte* (1677)

I

Racine took two years to write *Phèdre*, and I took two years to
adapt it for the English stage. My methods, such as they are, a
mixture of what Dryden called metaphrase and paraphrase, are
no more original than Johnson's *Vanity of Human Wishes* or than
Racine's who made his play out of the Greek of Euripides and the
Latin of Seneca, as well as earlier dramatic versions of the myth in
his own tongue. In a pre-Romantic age I would feel little need for
self-justification, nor feel I need be defensive about the poet's role
as adapter. Nothing better could be said on that issue than what
was written by Lion Feuchtwanger in his poem 'Adaptations'
(1924) composed after collaborating with Brecht on their version
of 'Edward II' *after* Marlowe:

> I, for instance, sometimes write
> Adaptations. Or some people prefer the phrase
> 'Based on', and this is how it is: I use
> Old material to make a new play, then
> Put under the title
> The name of the dead writer who is extremely
> Famous and quite unknown, and before
> The name of the dead writer I put the little word 'After'.
> Then one group will write that I am
> Very respectful and others that I am nothing of the sort and all
> The dead writer's failures
> Will be ascribed
> To me and all my successes
> To the dead writer who is extremely
> Famous and quite unknown, and of whom

[v]

Nobody knows whether he himself
Was the writer or maybe the
Adapter.

Critics of *Phaedra Britanica* have provided a spectrum of opinion as wide and as contradictory as that in the Feuchtwanger poem, from the English critic (to whom Racine was, no doubt, 'quite unknown') who accused me of taking a 'crowbar' to the original, to the French critic Jean-Jacques Gautier writing in *Le Figaro* and finding that in my version 'la noblesse linéaire, la flamme, la grandeur de l'ouvrage original est préservée.'

II

When a play becomes a 'vehicle' only, the greater part of it has died. If we go to see *Phèdre*, wrote Roland Barthes, it's on account of a particular great actress, a certain number of felicitous lines, some famous *tirades* set against a background of obscurity and boredom. We tolerate the rest. Barthes was writing after the production by Jean Vilar at the TNP in 1957 with Maria Casarès, and his reluctant conclusion was prominently displayed in the programme of a production I saw in Paris in 1974 at the Theatre Essaion: *'Je ne sais pas s'il est possible de jouer Racine aujourd'hui. Peut-être sur scene ce théatre est-il aux trois-quart mort.'* Similarly Jean-Louis Barrault in his *Mise en scene de Phèdre* (1946) writes that audiences went to see Sarah Bernhardt as Phèdre, but they didn't go to see the *piece*. They didn't even go to see the divine Sarah in the *entire* role, but the two scenes in which she excelled the declaration of Act II and the despair of Act IV. *'Phèdre n'est pas un concerto pour femme,'* Barrault warns us, *'mais une symphonie pour orchestre d'acteurs'.* The solution to the problem offered by Barrault could well apply to the revival of any classic play that has become simply a one role play by coming adrift from its social origins: *'Phèdre femme doit de nouveau s'incorporer dans Phèdre tragédie.'* A play is 'about' everyone who sets foot on the stage, principals and mutes alike. The way to re-energize *Phèdre*, setting aside for the moment the well nigh insuperable problems of doing that for an English audience, is to

[vi]

rediscover a *social* structure which makes the tensions and polarities of the play significant again. To make the roles, neglected for the sake of the 'vehicle' role, meaningful again. To grasp the *play* entire. It is only when the characters around her are duly re-instated that the central figure can be seen in her true light. One can begin by going back to the title displayed on the original edition of Racine's text in 1677: *Phèdre et Hippolyte*. In order to correct the theatrical imbalance and sharpen the focus, one needs such, perhaps overloaded, assertions as Leo Spitzer's that Thésée is the most important person in the play. He is after all left alive with the awareness of the consequence of his actions, and the knowledge of the deaths of his wife and son. He has the last word.

III

There is a mode of literary criticism, built upon the ruins of neo-classicism, and deriving from a period which was beginning to value intensity of experience at the expense of structure, a mode of criticism that extracts the principle 'beauties' of a work, Arnoldian 'touchstones', as though the essence of poetry resided in a few reverberant lines, and long works like Homer's were nothing more than a handful of titillating monosticha, rooted out of grey unappealing tracts by Romantic truffle-hounds. It's an attitude represented at its extreme by Poe's opinion that 'there is no such thing as a long poem.' It made assayer Matthew Arnold call Dryden and Pope 'classics of our *prose*'. Racine has suffered similarly in France. Henri de Montherlant thought that there were only twenty-seven lines of 'poetry' in the whole *oeuvres* of Racine, some 20,000 lines. Jean Dutourd thought that Racine's Alexandrines were ninety-nine per cent. rhetoric and one per cent. 'poetry'. One line which has consistently seemed to glitter from all this dross is one which Flaubert thought the most beautiful line in the whole of French Literature, and which Proust valued for its *beauté dénuée de sens*. It's a line which, typically, can only be understood, like most of Arnold's rhapsodical nuggets, by referring it back to the total context from which it was prised, by reconstructing the strata from which it was hastily lifted. One has to assume the responsibility of the archaeologist among so many opportunist treasure seekers. The line in question is the famous one spoken by Hippolyte describing Phèdre as

La fille de Minos et de Pasiphaé

Admittedly it is a crucial line. A line full of mythical reverberations. For those who know the myth. And it's not enough to refer the *reader*, as most French editions do, to the *tableau généologique* or the *index mythologique*. For one thing we are preparing a piece for the stage and not the study. Tableaus and indices are not theatrical, at least in a would-be Racinian recreation. The line is the key to the inner struggle of Phèdre, to her essential torment. For those who are at home in the obscure genealogies of Crete. As eighteenth century commentators puts it, this line *'semble préparer le spectateur à ce caractère mélangé de vices et de remords que le poète donne a Phèdre.'* The key word in this is *mélangé*. Many simply stress that the line signals the bad heredity of Phèdre, as if it were simply a case of the mother, Pasiphaë, though R. C. Knight tentatively suggests that 'Minos *may* perhaps stand for moral conscience'. Both elements of Phèdre's parentage are of equal importance. The problem about expanding the line, and absorbing into it the facts given in study texts by genealogies impossible to project theatrically, is that the line occurs in a context of nervous reticence. It is an old story for Hippolyte and Théramène. Théramène cuts off Hippolyte with an abrupt *'J'entends'*. The line foreshadows the causes of Phèdre's shame and her need to break through the barriers of shame; it articulates her tension, without Hippolyte having to transgress his own sense of propriety by being specific. It is an 'enough said' situation. The polarities represented by Minos and Pasiphaë are those which maintain the tension of the whole play and not simply the character of Phèdre. Minos and Pasiphaë, an emblematical marriage, are the opposite poles of the human consciousness. Minos (whose function we cannot ignore and who is given a disastrously misleading emphasis in Robert Lowell's epithet 'homicidal') is one of the three judge figures in Greek mythology.

He is the judge who *punishes* crime, as opposed to Aeacus, who represents division of property, and Rhadamantus, the rewarder of virtue. Interiorized psychologically, as he is in Phèdre, he is that part of our selves which is judgement, prescription, that part that creates moral codes, imposes laws, fixes limites, the 'frontiers' of experience, defines the acceptable, and punishes transgression. pasiphaë is the transgressor of the codes created by Minos, that part of our selves that hungers for every experience, burns to go beyond the frontiers of current acceptability, specifically, in her case, to gratify her sexuality with a bull, incur the guilt of forbidden bestiality. She is what Henri de Montherlant made of her in his play *Pasiphaé* (1928), the woman who wants to transcend morality, accept *every* part of her nature, however 'animal' or 'bestial' it has been branded by the law-makers, to assert that nothing is unhealthy or forbidden. She rejects the codes of her husband Minos. The Minos/Pasiphaë duality is yet another statement of 'civilization and its discontents'. In that sense we are all children of Minos and Pasiphaë. The wedlock of Minos and Pasiphaë is a dynamic power struggle for the upper hand fraught with matrimonial tension, uneasy even in brief armistice. The struggle lives on in their daughter Phèdre with the father Minos continually more assertive. I have isolated the function of Minos, and made him simply 'the Judge', who represents internally the moral conscience, and is, in the exterior political world, a representative of 'the rule of reason', like the ambiguously placed Governor himself, only utterly unimpeachable:

> a judge so unimpeacheable and just
> to have a wife destroyed by bestial lust!

That may well seem a far cry from the cherished

> La fille de Minos et de Pasiphaé

and it is not intended as its formal equivalent. I have had to redistribute the energies of that renowned line over my whole version, surrender the more obvious nugget for a concession to work the whole seam more painstakingly.

The problem, then, of Phèdre, as of us all, is that she contains within herself both Minos *and* Pasiphaë. That is the essence of the genealogy. She condemns the mother/female/accepter/'transgressor' in herself with the voice of the father/the male voice of punishment/repression/rigid social code. That is the psychological dynamic of the character. As with the outer political dynamic I have sought to create an equivalent, but redistributed, nexus of imagery for the internal tensions. The 'bestiality' of Pasiphaë is seen as part of the threat of the alien, of that personified, often apostrophized INDIA upon which the exiled British projected all that was forbidden in their own culture. The temple sculpture and painting of India depicts in a spirit of acceptance, what one particular picture reproduced in the National Theatre programme for *Phaedra Britannica*, called 'the love of all creatures'. It is a painting from Rajasthan of circa 1780 showing not only pairs of animals copulating but women in joyful congress with a variety of beasts. One could well apply to it the long passage of the power of Venus from Seneca's *Phaedra*:

> The dolphin of the raging sea doth love:
> the elephants by Cupid's blaze do burn:
> Dame Nature all doth challenge as her own,
> And nothing is that can escape her laws:

That in the translation of John Studley, 1581, the first English version of Seneca's play. But the Indian picture goes just a little further, extends the frontiers of Venus into bestiality. This is quite beyond the limits of acceptability for the British in India, totally alien, though no doubt present in the dark recesses of the imagination. To Western eyes India seemed actually to celebrate a world where everything was sexually possible. The Western reaction was both fascinated (Pasiphaë) and repressive (Minos). It is the voice of Minos we hear speaking through Lieutenant General Sir George MacMunn:

> In the description of the astounding indecency which to Western eyes the temples of Conjeveram, of Jaganath and the Black Pagoda offer, mention has been made of the bestiality recorded: the mingling of humans and animals in intimate embrace. . . . The ancient religions did permit such terrible abominations and India has always apparently been more openly aquainted with such matters than the rest of the world.

[x]

When the guilt of Pasiphaë, which, it should be noted, is never specifically referred to in Racine, although it is, characteristically, in Seneca, is mentioned in my version it is intended with reference to what is depicted in the temples listed by Sir George MacMunn:

> Mother! Driven by the dark gods' spite
> beyond the frontiers of appetite!
> A *judge*'s wife! Obscene! Such bestialities
> Hindoos might sculpture on a temple frieze.

And the monster which kills Thomas Theophilus (Hippolyte) and seems to represent the suppressed passions of all the principle characters is described by Burleigh as being

> like one of those concoctions that one sees
> in dark recesses on a temple frieze.

But on the faces of the women in the painting from Rajasthan, women being joyfully pleasured by everything from a peacock to an elephant we have the spirit of Pasiphaë seeking the total joy that seems to lie beyond all remorse and moral codes. One senses the Yeatsian cry:

> When such as I cast out remorse
> So great a sweetness flows into the breast
> We must laugh and we must sing,
> We are blest by everything
> Everything we look upon is blest.

The nearest my Memsahib ever gets to understanding such a mood is, ironically, in her envy of the young lovers, she imagines untrammelled by the agonies that destroy her:

> To follow one's feelings through nature's course
> without recriminations and remorse,
> not to feel criminal, and meet as though
> the sun shone on one's love and watched it grow!
> Ah! Every day they must wake up and see
> vistas with no black clouds, and feel so free!

The tensions of the Minos/Pasiphaë polarity are maintained too in my images of the hunter, the Victorian type, projecting his inner repressed desires on to the fauna of India, amassing tigerpelts,

[xi]

covering his walls with animal heads, collecting obsessive proof that he is in control of his own animal nature, that he is the fit representative of 'the rule of reason'. The Governor himself is renowned as a great hunter, naturally, often scorning the rifle with its distant rationally controlled despatch for closer gladiatorial combat with a bayonet. The images of the hunt are maintained, in one degree or another, in all the versions of the story: Euripides, Seneca. Racine. At the beginning of the Euripides play Aphrodite (Venus) herself complains of Hippolytus not only that he denies her by ignoring women but also by driving wild animals off the face of the earth (ἐξαιρει χθονος κυσὶν ταχέιαις θῆρας). Venus, the principle of generation, replenishes the stocks exhausted by the hunter. The nurse in Seneca tells the destructively chaste young man as much, imagining the world as an unpopulated desert without the influence of the love goddess:

> Excedat, agedum, rebus humanis Venus,
> Quae supplet ac restituit exhaustum genus;
> Orbis iacebit squallido turpis situ;
> Vacuum sine ullis classibus stabit mare;
> Alesque coelo deerit, & silvis fera;

(469-473)

The first speech of the Seneca play is one in praise of the excitement of hunting and a list of quarry. Ironically one of the beasts listed — 'latis feri cornibus uri', probably some sort of buffalo, is described in an edition of 1902 as 'extinct' owing to the untiring perseverance of the hunter! There is another element to the obsessive animal slaying. What is part of human nature, but not acknowledged, tends to be labelled 'animal'. Even in today's papers behaviour which does not even transcend the limits of acceptability as much as Pasiphaë's is labelled by the Minos voice of judgement from the British bench as 'animal' or 'bestial'. We are very nervous of our status on what used to be called 'the scale of Creation'. And this is the point of the animal abuse with which the Memsahib finally rejects her 'lower' self in the shape of her ayah, or with which the Governor denounces Thomas Theophilus, when he tries to reimpose *within* his household the rigid limits he himself has clearly gone beyond outside the home.

[xii]

The Governor's own position on this shifting scale of trans-gression and animality, with Minos at one end and Pasiphaë at the other, is decidedly ambiguous. The Governor both accepts and represses, he is both law and transgression. He is in many ways the classic male hypocrite. He avidly seeks experience outside the limits of his own code, or the code his society ostensibly subscribes to, but to do so he finds it necessary, as to many Victorians did, to adopt 'native costume'. Sir Richard Burton is only one of the most well known of models for such behaviour. In some ways the Governor carries the whole burden of the male Victorian dilemma. I wanted to state the conflict at a social and political level as well as at the psychological, as it is in Racine in slightly different form. Another redistribution. I took the clues for this from what the Victorian imagination found not only in its Indian experience, but also in its assessment of the Theseus legend itself. All ages have used the long surviving classical heroes like Odysseus, Aeneas, Theseus to realize their own natures and pre-occupations. W. B. Standford's *The Ulysses Theme* has charted the fortunes of Odysseus from Homer to Joyce, and Anne C. Ward's *The Quest for Theseus* (Pall Mall Press, London, 1970) has done more or less the same for the hero of our present play. To the Victorians who often cast themselves into the roles of classical heroes reborn, Theseus was a type of Victorian. John Ruskin in Letter XXII dated 1872 of *Fors Clavigera* sees in Theseus:

'. . . the great settler or law-giver of the Athenian state; but he is so eminently as the Peace-Maker, causing men to live in fellowship who before lived separate, and making roads passable that had been infested with robbers and wild beasts. He is that exterminator of every bestial and savage element.'

With this as a guide one may specify merely from those combats with monsters, grotesques, giants and brigands that Racine uses:

> Les monstres étouffés et les brigands punis,
> Procuste, Cercyon, et Scirron et Sinnis,
> Et les os dispersés du géant d'Epidaure,
> Et la Crete fumant du sang du Minotaure.

The accounts of early 'law-giving', the establishment of 'the rule of

[xiii]

law' in British India read like a British version of the same kind of heroic, semi-mythical exploit. And not simply the obvious sources like Sleeman's account of the suppression of Thugee, legendary brigands and murderers worthy of any Theseus, but others mentioned always in mythologizing tones by, for example, James Douglas in his *Bombay & Western India* (1893): 'England is the St George that has slain the great dragon of infanticide which among the Jhadejas ravaged Kach and Kathiawar'. 'Jauhar, that Cyclopean monster of self-immolation', 'the Hashashin' (from whom we derive our word assassin), 'Dacoits', 'Aghori Cannibals', 'the anthropophagous Mardicura'. Douglas is also typical also when he dramatizes in a mythological almost hagiographical way the tiger-slaughter of, for example, Sir James Outram, who in ten years was present at the deaths of 191 tigers, 15 leopards, 25 bears and 12 buffaloes. He doesn't mention what Aphrodite thought of Sir James Outram but he hails him as 'another St Paul, (he) had been a day and a night in the deep and fought with wild beasts'. 'The wild beasts and wilder men' of accounts like Douglas's of the establishing of 'the rule of law' in British India represent the same stage of civilization of the Greece before Theseus, and the Victorians saw their own confrontation in his. So the Governor in *Phaedra Britannica* is, as John Ruskin wrote, 'that exterminator of every bestial or savage element', but, at the same time, he is also, as someone called Sir Richard Burton 'an authority on all that relates to the bestial element in man'. This authority is acquired, of course, as the Governor, who represents 'the rule of reason' and suppresses alien bestiality, while, at the same time, as his other ('lower') self he explores his own animality in his forays 'in native costume'. It is with these two contrasting elements in his father that Thomas Theophilus has to struggle. In an article in *MacMillan's Magazine* for August 1889 Walter Pater adds an important qualification to a summary of the character of Theseus that, in other respects, is similar to Ruskin's. His Theseus:

'. . . figures, passably, as a kind of mythic shorthand for civilization, making roads and the like, facilitating travel, suppressing various forms of violence, *but many innocent things as well.*'

[xiv]

As law-giver, then, Theseus/Thésée/the Governor shares an element of repression with the father of Phaedra/Phèdre/the Memsahib. But only part. The other side of his nature, the seeker of new experiences, especially sexual, often 'in disguise' precisely because he cannot relate the two halves of his nature, goes hand in hand with the hunter of beasts and the supressor of bestial custom. That which he is most fascinated by he represses most ruthlessly. He is a kind of mythic shorthand, if you like, for civilization *and* its discontents.

The Khan who imprisons the Governor in my version of 'a season spent in Hell' lies, on this scale of transgression, somewhere between the Governor and Pasiphaë. There is even a slight note of envy perhaps in these lines of the Governor's:

> My captor was a beast, obscene, perverse,
> given to practises I won't rehearse,
> to crude carnalities that overrode
> every natural law and human code.
> He'd draw the line at nothing, no taboo
> would stop him doing what he wanted to.

The Governor has gone beyond 'the frontier' both geographically and psychologically. Some of the vocabulary of territory from our Anglo-Indian experience marks the boundaries very well. 'The frontiers of appetite . . . of virtue . . . of blood.' The Governor has gone beyond 'the frontier', beyond the Indus, known every-where as 'the forbidden river'. H. Bosworth Smith in his *Life of Lord Lawrence* speaks of the Khyber Pass as 'the forbidden precincts over whose gloomy portals might well have been inscribed the words of Dante:

> All hope abandon, ye who enter here

So the hellish overtones, the Stygian symbolism were created for me by those with some historical experience of the Anglo-Indian period I chose for my setting. Whatever the Governor has experienced, and he is, possibly through fear or shame, vaguely unspecific, he has finally seen the limits of the acceptable. His version of hell is being subjected to another's unlimited will, and suffering in the way that many victims of his casual sexual whims

[xv]

might well have suffered. His experience is a vision of the monstrous, the non-human other, beyond all human access and control, even for a 'law-giver', something more terrible than mere animal or beast, something that cannot finally be suppressed or mounted on a Residency wall, nor even physically embraced. This monster defeats both Minos and Pasiphaë. A monster to whom victims must be fed. ('Is there not a home among us that has not paid blood tribute to that relentless monster', writes an Anglo-Indian lady, meaning India). The Governor's vision is probably a glimpse of the monster that finally destroys his son. Whatever the experience he has had of hell it is one which makes him long for the circumscribed, apparently ordered world of his marriage and home. But the boundaries of that he finds are now shaken, the barriers in need of reconstruction, the edges blurred between inner and outer, hell and earth . . .

> A season spent in hell, I've no desire
> for whiffs of brimstone from the household fire.

IV

Neoclassical plays are about sex and politics. From as early as classical times there has been a healthily vulgar if slightly overdone satiric scorn for Phaedra's problems. The taboo of incest between stepmother and stepson seems irrelevant in societies with different kinship restraints. It is easy for us to feel self-satisfied at what we think of as our own permissiveness and to sneer at sexual problems which were at the time agonizingly real. If literature is, what Ezra Pound said it was 'news that stays news' then dramatic agony should stay agony, but this is difficult when the tensions involved have come adrift from their social origins. To Ovid, the Roman poet of sexual opportunism, Phaedra's passion was not only not incestuous, Hippolytus had to be chivvied by her beyond *his* consciousness of taboo:

> Nec, quia privigno videar coitura noverca
>   Terruerint animos nomina vana tuos
> Ista vetus pietas, aevo moritura futuro,
>   Rustica Saturno regno tenente fuit.
>   (Phaedra Hippolito — *Heroides* III)

[xvi]

And this in the translation of poet/dramatist Thomas Otway who
also did a version of Racine's *Bérénice* into heroic couplets:

> How can'st thou reverence thy Father's Bed,
> From which himself so Abjectly is fled?
> The thought affrights not me, but me enflames;
> Mother and Son are notions, very Names
> Of Worn out Piety, in Fashion Then
> When old dull *Saturn* rul'd the Race of men.
> But braver Jove taught pleasure was no sin,
> And with his sister did himself begin.

These attitudes to a 'worn out Piety', repeated often enough
throughout the ages, are mild enough compared with a version of
the story published only five years after Racine's play in Alexander
Radcliffe's *Terrestrial Hymns & Carnal Ejaculations* (1682). This
is a Phaedra Britannica, isolated in 'a Farm-House in Putney in
Surrey' who has no feelings of restraint whatsoever, either
Euripidean Greek or neoclassical French:

> When Young, I cou'd have cur'd these am'rous stings
> With Carrots, Radishes, or such like things;
> Now there's no pleasure in such Earthly cures,
> I must have things apply'd as warm as yours.
> Where lies the blame, art thou not strong, and young?
> Who would not gather fruit that is well hung?

In this case Pasiphaë has triumphed over Minos, and reworking
the passage already quoted from Ovid and Otway, Radcliffe has:

> Wee'd no such opportunity before:
> Your Father is at London with his Whore.
> Therefore I think 'tis but a just design,
> To cuckold him, and pay him in his coin.
> Besides he ne're was marry'd to your Mother,
> He first whor'd her, and then he took another.
> What kindness or respect ought we to have
> For such a Villain and perfidious Knave?
> This should not trouble, but provoke us rather
> With all the speed we can to lye together.
> I am no kin to you, nor you to me,

They call it Incest but to terrifie.
Lovers Embraces are Lascivious Tricks
'Mongst musty Puritans and Schismaticks.

This is that 'Anglo-Saxon irreverence' that Michael Billington mentioned in his review of *Phaedra Britannica*. One sees it too in Stevie Smith's poem *Phèdre*. And very necessary it is too though it scarcely helps to recreate the Racinian mode in modern English. We read such pieces in early rehearsals, partly for the couplets, but also to draw the fire of cheerful vulgarity before we tackled the main text. It's an irreverence not confined to our attitude to in-accessible foreign classics, and I associate it in my mind with one of my culture heroes, the comedian 'Prof.' Leon Cortez, who offered his own cockneyfications of Shakespeare, reducing the high flown poetry of kings to an earthy demotic. Nor is such irreverence, purely Anglo-Saxon, even towards Racine. Far from it. In June 1974 I saw a production of *Phèdre* I have already referred to, directed by Régis Santon at the Theatre Essaion, which played the Racinian text as vulgar farce, a compound of Bunuel, Racine and Feydeau, with Tristan and Isolde as background music, and a vaguely Latin American setting, some-thing like Torre Nilsson's film *La Casa del Angel*. The production had simply given up the struggle to present the play on its own terms, and enjoyable as it was as a lively piece of juvenile iconoclasm, very necessary for the French classic theatre, it gave no help whatsoever to one desperately seeking access to the play for equally, if not more, irreverent English audiences. With this constant sense of total subversion I had, even more carefully, to consider solutions to the play which would place the problem in a society where the sense of transgression was once more an agonizing burden. Sexual problems do not occur in a vacuum, in a theatrical never-never land, but are created by social codes. The period I chose eventually, after many false-starts and crablike researches, envisaged a particular society, early Victorian Britain, with a rigid code made even more formally defensive by being placed in the alien environs of sensual India.

The politics of the play are also obscured by genealogical com-plications, with which we no longer have any spontaneous rapport, and distanced by our distaste for the absolute monarchy of the

[xviii]

court of Louis XIV. Even the translator cannot shirk his responsibility for historical criticism.

Everywhere in the imagery of seventeenth century poetry, prose and drama, in England and France, the psychological structure of man is seen as an interiorization of the political. 'The Government of Man' writes the Cambridge Platonist, Benjamin Whichcote, 'should be the Monarchy of Reason; it is too often a Democracy of Passions'. Passions are elsewhere in Dryden

> unreasonable things
> That strike at Sense, as Rebels do at Kings.

When Dryden came to paraphrase the famous Latin hymn *Veni Creator Spiritus* the simple lines:

> infirma nostri corporis
> virtue firmans perpeti

become a typical piece of the politically expressed psychology I mean:

> Our Frailties help, our vice controul;
> Submit the Senses to the Soul;
> And when Rebellious they are grown
> Then lay thy hand and hold 'em down.

The alignment of political synonyms in such imagery is: Reason/King/Rule/Monarchy/(to which series we can add *raj*=rule) on the one hand and what they restrain on the other: Passions/Mob/Democracy/('the Natives'). As Martin Turnell, the best English commentator on Racine, points out: 'there are only two classes in Racine: masters and servants, the rulers and the ruled, royalty and the people'. Elsewhere discussing the psychology of Corneille and Racine he writes that 'reason has to operate *tyrannically* and repress by force an uprush of the senses'. Hence 'the rule of law'; the use of words like 'seditious' and 'mutinous' of the passions. hence also the time of the piece, defined as taking place a few years before the Mutiny. As I used the prospect of 'les événements' of 1968 in Paris as a political, historical 'measure' of the realities of my setting of *Le Misanthrope* and of Alceste's status as a critic of society, so in *Phaedra Britannica* I imagine the tensions of the play continuing into the Indian Mutiny, 1857, (the year also of the

Obscene Publications Act.) My text demands that the political realities of Racinian society are reinterpreted physically, realized literally in 'black and white'. I sought to re-energize critically the political content by aligning it with the British 'Imperial dream', which like Goya's dream of reason, 'produces monsters'.

V

Aphrodite speaks in Euripides. In Seneca Venus is merely addressed. But even in Euripides the gods are, as his translator Philip Vellacott puts it, 'no more than dramatic fictions'. The gods in Racine, as Martin Turnell points out, are 'projections of basic human impulses which means that in *Phèdre* they belong to the realm of psychology rather than theology'. 'Venus, c'est Phèdre, c'est Hippolyte . . . Neptune est dans Thésée,' writes Jean-Louis Barrault in his production notes. The British projected their own suppressed nature on to the continent they subdued, personifying a destructive INDIA, devastating to those who gave in to its powers, who were seduced by its nakedly obvious allure. Personification is general throughout the literature and memoirs of British India. Everything psychologically alien or suppressed becomes 'India' or 'the dark gods' or, not detached enough to be theologically accurate, an apostrophized Hindu deity like Siva or some other menacing god from a bewilderingly diverse pantheon. Here, for example, is an Englishwoman writing about the 'Hot Weather':

> One has to experience the coming of the Hot Season to understand something of the worship of Siva — Creator and Destroyer — the Third Person of the Hindu Trinity. For its approach — swift, relentless and inevitable — is like that of a living and sensate force — like the visible work of that terrible yet withal beneficent God who destroys and tramples all things beneath His feet in an ecstatic harmonious dance, that He may create them anew. For in a sense there is a necessity for the hot weather. The intensity of the sun's power cracks and cleaves the dry, obdurate earth, in order ·that the blessed rains of the Monsoon may irrigate and revivify the whole, jaded, exhausted face of the land.

And as Jean-Louis Barrault speaks of the tragedy of *Phèdre*,

[xx]

giving the arc and carthartic trajectory of the play the same kind of cumulative, meteorological image, as 'un de ces orages de fin aout', it seems to make Siva, as present in the British imagination, particularly fitted to preside over the passion of *Phaedra Britannica*. The same woman goes on to describe her feelings of helplessness in the Indian heat (which another woman Mrs E. M. Croker likens to some 'cruel vindictive animal') in terms which, typically, create the sense of powerful alien forces:

> And finally there is the close, hot evening, and an airless night of tossing and turning, of trying to find one cool spot in one's bed, giving it up in despair, and lying in still resignation to look up at the uncaring stars above the gently flapping punkah, helpless beneath the destroying feet of Siva.

Such projections on to an alien divinity are very common in Anglo-Indian writing, and they tend to stand for those things that are felt to be outside the sphere of reason, order and justice (or the current concepts of them) which it is the function of tragedy, according to George Steiner, to reveal as 'terribly limited'. It was to insist on the role of the gods as projections that I conflated the functions of Venus and Neptune in Racine. The sea which in Racine is the symbol of the uncontrolled, the formless, becomes in my version 'the jungle' almost a synonym for chaos. I have unified the psychological projections represented in Racine and ascribed them both to Siva, as he was imagined by the British, not necessarily as a complex component of the Hindu pantheon. Contemplating the attributes of Siva, though, one can see that the god can well bear the parallels, being at once the god of regeneration and sexuality, and of destruction. He contains opposing forces. He is associated both with aescetism (Hippolyte) and yet is everywhere reverenced under the symbol of the phallus or *lingam*. He Destroyer/Creator, birth and death, Apollo *and* Dionysus to use the Nietzschean pair that forge the tragic dialectic. Even the minor parallels can be maintained, to authenticate the transfer, as Siva has a bull as a vehicle, and as a weapon the *trisula* or trident. But the matchings at this level hardly matter, even if they aid the metamorphosis. What matters is the function of projection, the use of pagan gods in a culture that dramatizes itself as an age of reason, and its

[xxi]

equivalent in the British apostrophization of the dark gods of India.

VI

I don't remember the exact point at which I decided on a nineteenth century Indian setting, but in retrospect there seem to have been catalysts and clues about me from the start, though I did begin with versions ostensibly in Ancient Greece and in the period of Louis XIV. Of all the many elements I now can recognize the following as particularly prominent:

1. Maria Casarès, who played Phèdre in Jean Vilar's production at the TNP in 1957 said of her character: *'j'ai toujours imaginée étendue dans l'ombre d'un chambre close, dans un lieu où le soleil explose'*. India! The all-pervading presence of the sun, either seen as light or felt as heat in a darkened room, became also a physical counterpart for Phèdre's mythological kinship in the original.

2. There was an equivalent, felt intuitively at first and then researched, between the way critics write about the character of the confidante, Oenone, and the way in which Anglo-Indian memoirs and fiction write of the ayah figure. Jean-Louis Barrault calls Oenone the 'valeur noire' of Phèdre, and in my version she is literally that (the Anglo-Indians used the inaccurate and deliberately insulting adjective 'black' of Indians). Racine also speaks, too aristocratically and high-handedly for my liking, of the *bassesse* of Oenone, and the servile propensities which make *her* able to accuse Hippolyte, and her not mistress as was the case in the Euripides version. As I have made it a Memsahib and ayah relationship, it is a way of absorbing into my version, without doing violence to the sense, my social reservations about Racine, and it makes the Memsahib's final outburst of racialist rejection of her faithful servant a terrible one, and one that is linked to the outside world of alien domination of which the psychological is a mirror aspect.

3. I felt the need of making the Amazon mother of Hippolyte physically present in the son, a constant reminder of the past of Thésée. My Hippolyte, Thomas Theophilus, becomes a 'half-

caste' embodying the tensions between Britain and India within himself, as much as he embodies the two conflicting selves of his father. The occurrence of marriage between British men and Indian women was by no means uncommon in nineteenth century India and, if we need historical authentication, it is enough to cite only the more well-known examples like James Achilles Kirkpatrick, Resident at Hyderabad, Job Charnock, who rescued a Brahmin widow from suttee and lived with her happily until her natural death fourteen years after, Colonel Gardiner, and Sir Charles Metcalfe who had three Eurasian sons by an Indian princess probably related to Ranjit Singh. The railways were to bring the Memsahibs to India and put a stop to that. I have assumed that transition in *mores* to be taking place, creating a new distance between ruler and ruled that was to harden to a more rigid *apartheid* after the Mutiny of 1857. The Victorian male couldn't permit his women the same intimate insights into India which he had allowed himself before his ladies made the crossing over the 'black water'.

4. Assailed as the British felt on all sides by an irrational India with its dark sensual gods and 'primitive' customs, they created in their imagination defensive roles for themselves as the inheritors of rational civilization. They constructed residencies and public buildings in classical style, attempting to realize in external marble what they felt unable to realize internally in their far from securely stable minds. The books of the period are full of engravings showing proud classical façades in clearings in dense jungle, with creeper and mangrove festooning the edges of the scene. It is an eloquent juxtaposition. Mark Bence-Jones in his *Palaces of the Raj* (London, 1973) describes the Residency at Hyderabad, with its Durbar Hall lined with Ionic columns, and a staircase which 'was adorned with sculpture: the Apollo Belvedere, Leda and the Swan' (not Pasiphaë and the Bull to complete the circle but almost there!) and 'Venus rising from the sea'. 'The mirrors in neo-classical frames, reflected the Durbar Hall to infinity.' It reads almost like the description of a traditional set for *Phèdre* at the *Comédie Française!*

It is more than a convenient point of contact. It represents the effort of one era, with its values threatened, to define itself in terms

[xxiii]

borrowed from another, which would seem best to support and prop up what was felt to be most shaky. The drama of Britain and India was constantly seen in these terms. Even as late as 1924 (the year of *A Passage to India*) Bennet Christian Huntingdon Calcraft Kennedy could write: 'we are here to govern India as delegates of a Christian and civilized power. We are here as representatives of Christ and Caesar to maintain this land against Siva and Khalifa'. And the cleaned-up classicism of the corresponding architecture, deriving as it does from Greece and Rome via Palladio and Wren, is still, as David Gerhard writing about Lutyens's New Delhi Residency, has it, 'a favourite political symbol in our century ranging from the megalomania of Albert Speer and Hitler to the New Deal of Roosevelt'. This belief in our being the chosen heirs of Greece and Rome gives a special poignancy to those pictures of the classical façade of the Lucknow Residency after the Mutiny, shattered by rifle-fire and shell, and littered with skulls. This kind of Residency and the life lived within it seemed to fit almost exactly Martin Turnell's summary of the dramatic and political function of the palace in the plays of Racine. They are 'not simply impersonal buildings which provide a setting for the tragedy . . . They represent a particular *order* . . .':

> We are aware from the first of an almost suffocating tension in the air combined with a desperate effort to maintain some sort of control which frequently breaks down. The tension is pervasive; it is also contagious. It is the atmosphere which produces fascinating and frightening revelations about human nature — about ourselves.
>
> The palaces vary in style . . . they have one thing in common. There is something of the prison about them. We have the impression that the community is somehow confined within their walls. The sense of confinement is partly psychological, but in some parts of the palaces we shall find one or two members of the community are literally prisoners . . .
>
> The palaces are huge, dark, claustrophobic. They give the occupants the alarming impression that they are constantly being watched, that their lives are in danger in that disaster may overtake at any moment.
>
> There are winding corridors with innumerable rooms leading

[xxiv]

off them. But we the visitors, are only admitted to a single room. The whole of the drama is concentrated inside it . . . at the same time we are aware that the room, or more accurately, the palace, is *a world within a world it is trying to dominate.*

(Jean Racine, Dramatist)

VII

Couplets keep the cat on the hot tin roof. Each spirit has its own custom-built treadmill. After the metronome, the comic pace-maker of *The Misanthrope* couplet, I wanted a more organic model for my iambics. I wanted to return the iamb back to its sources in breath and blood. In the silences one should hear the heart beat. Jean-Louis Barrault writing of the Alexandrine in *Phèdre* says:

> le coeur, qui egrène, jusqu'a la mort, les deux temps de son tam tam obsédant: systole-diastole; systole-diastole. Breve-longue; breve-longue etc: *le coeur bat l'iambe.*

It was this heartbeat, this bloodthrob that marked the time of my metric. The heart as 'tam-tam obsédant' leads us straight back too to British India, where another woman writes in her memoir, 'the throbbing tom-toms became almost like our heartbeats':

> I sensed the gods of India were there
> behind the throbbing heat and stifling air.
> Heart beat like a tom-tom, punkah flapped
> backwards and forwards and my strength was sapped.
> I felt you mocking, India, you brewed
> strange potions out of lust and lassitude,
> dark gods mocking, knowing they can claim
> another woman with the Judge's name,
> picking off the family one by one,
> each destroyed by lust and Eastern sun.

Newcastle-upon-Tyne
November 1975   TONY HARRISON

All photographs by Anthony Crickmay

1 The Governor's Wife *(Diana Rigg)*

2 Ayah *(Alaknanda Samarth)*
Burleigh *(Robert Eddison)*

3 Thomas Theophilus *(David Yelland)*
  Lilamani *(Diana Quick)*

4 The Governor's Wife *(Diana Rigg)*

5 Ayah *(Alaknanda Samarth)*
The Governor's Wife *(Diana Rigg)*

6 *left to right* Servant *(Jagdish Kumar)*, A.D.C. *(Daniel Thorndike)*, Chuprassie *(Ishaq Bux)*, Servant *(Albert Moses)*, Burleigh *(Robert Eddison)*, Thomas Theophilus *(David Yelland)*.

Governor *(Michael Gough)*, Ayah *(Alaknanda Samarth)*, The Governor's Wife *(Diana Rigg)*

7 The Governor's Wife *(Diana Rigg)*
Governor *(Michael Gough)*

Phaedra Britannica was first performed by the
National Theatre Company at the Old Vic on
9 September 1975 with the following cast:

THE GOVERNOR	Michael Gough
THE GOVERNOR'S WIFE	Diana Rigg
THOMAS THEOPHILUS, THE GOVERNOR'S SON BY HIS FIRST WIFE	David Yelland
BURLEIGH, HIS TUTOR	Robert Eddison
ADC TO THE GOVERNOR	Daniel Thorndike
LILAMANI	Diana Quick
TARA, HER ATTENDANT	Illona Linthwaite
AYAH	Alaknanda Samarth
CHUPRASSIE	Ishaq Bux
SERVANTS	Talat Hussain
	Jagdish Kumar
	Albert Moses

DIRECTOR	John Dexter
DESIGNER	Tanya Moiseiwitsch
ASSISTANT TO THE DESIGNER	Timian Alsaker
LIGHTING	Andy Phillips
STAFF DIRECTOR	Harry Lomax
VOCAL COACH	Catherine Fleming
PRODUCTION MANAGER	Richard Bullimore
STAGE MANAGER	Diana Boddington
DEPUTY STAGE MANAGER	John Caulfield
ASSISTANT STAGE MANAGERS	Tim Spring
	Karen Stone
SOUND	Sylvia Carter

Note:
In the text / means *inhale* and
X *exhale*.

for
John Dexter
again

ACT ONE

The scene is the Durbar Hall of the Governor's Residency in British India, a few years before the Indian Mutiny. Thomas Theophilus and Burleigh stand behind the classical colonnade inhaling what is left of the fresh night air, and listening to the bugle from the Fort off-stage playing reveille.

THOMAS   No! No! I can't. *I can't.* How can I stay?
        I've got to go at once. At once. *Today!*
        The Governor's been gone now half a year,
        I can't stay loitering and loafing here
        frustrated and ashamed I'm not the one
        directing the search-parties, me, his son!
        It's almost up, the dawn. I must prepare.
BURLEIGH   And where will you start looking? Where?
        The Company's had sepoys scour as far
        as Jalalabad and Peshawar
        north to the very outposts where its *raj*
        is constantly beset by sabotage.
        Unpacified child-murdering marauders
        make it a certain death to cross our borders.
        You know the Governor! He might have strayed
        into those areas still unsurveyed.
        Thomas, you know as well as I that soon
        the search 'll be called off for the monsoon.
        Could even come today, the first cloudburst.
        This damned hot weather's at its very worst.
        Who wouldn't give a coffer of rupees
        to lower the mercury a few degrees?
        Besides, perhaps for reasons of his own
        H.E. prefers his whereabouts unknown.
        One knows his nature, ready to pursue
        anything that's savage, strange, or new,

[1]

his 'curiosity' how wild tribes live,
his 'scholar's' passion for the primitive.
Frankly it would be no great surprise
if he were living somewhere in disguise,
and, cool as ever, 's ready to embark
on some fresh enterprise that's best kept dark,
absorbed, preoccupied both day, *and* night,
lets say 'researching' some strange marriage rite!
Leading some new unfortunate astray!

THOMAS Show some respect. Be careful what you say!
Father's the Governor. He's good. He's great,
no loose romancer and gross reprobate.
My father's in some danger and not caught
in any trammels of that trivial sort.
When he was new out here and young, perhaps
there *was* the occasional moral lapse.
Not now, though, Burleigh. All that's of the past.
The Governor's heart is constant and steadfast.
No footloose fancy. No inconstant vow.
His life revolves round 'the Memsahib' now.
I'm going for two reasons: one, to find
my father; two, leave *this place* far behind.

BURLEIGH 'This place!' 'This place?' O surely that's not how
your childhood paradise seems to you now?
If 'this place', as you call it, 's lost its savour
where else I wonder will you find to favour?
Not Britain. No! Completely unimpressed!
There all you felt was homesick and depressed.
What's the real reason why you want to go?
Fear? Of what? Surely you can let me know!

THOMAS Yes, Burleigh, paradise it may have been . . .
until 'the Memsahib' came on the scene.
The Judge's daughter's presence soon destroyed
that carefree, tranquil life we all enjoyed . . .
a judge so unimpeachable and just
to have a wife destroyed by bestial lust
and daughters . . .

BURLEIGH   Yes. Indeed. Of course one knew

[2]

that things were far from well between you two.
The storybook stepson/stepmother thing!
She wasn't long in starting harassing.
No sooner had she seen you, you were sent
to school in Britain i.e. banishment!
That particular storm's blown over though.
The old obsession's gone, or doesn't show.
Besides it seems his Excellency's wife
has quite succumbed and lost all hold on life.
Her nerves seem whittled down to fiddle strings.
She's given in and lost all grip on things.
What happened to the mother years before 's
enough to give alarm for much less cause.
The India, we'd all like to ignore
struck at the Judge's family twice before,
bestial India, that undermined
his own wife's body and first daughter's mind.
Now she won't eat, can't sleep, and seems in pain,
though what it is no one can ascertain.
As to it's nature she's quite sealed her lips.
A very strange complaint her Ladyship's,
Not common fever with its heat and chills
but one of India's obscurer ills.
How can an ailing woman cause your flight?

THOMAS It's not the Memsahib. Or her vain spite.
(pause)
Remember the revolt? Ranjit and six sons
so bloodily destroyed by redcoat guns?
The daughter of that line that raised the war
against the Company and rule of law
under the strict restraint of house arrest . . .
She's the reason . . .

BURLEIGH   Come! Can you detest
poor Lilamani so much, you as well
as the Governor want her life made hell?
And she so innocent! Would she have known
about her father's plans to seize the throne?
I don't believe she knew about their plot

to overthrow the Sahibs. Surely not!
Politics! Rebellion! I don't suppose
she's even acquainted with words like those.
She seems so full of charm. At least to me.

THOMAS If it were hatred, would I need to flee?

BURLEIGH A little tentative analysis
from me, your oldest friend, can't come amiss.
I've watched you struggling, I know for you
the Governor's character's not one, but two.
As law-enforcer, hunter; fine! But pride
has hardened your nature to his 'darker' side.
How long for I wonder? Are you still
fighting off love's *raj* with iron will?
India's spirits stung by your disgust
will never rest until you've kissed the dust.
And blood will out! Have the dark gods won?
And are you, after all, your father's son?
I've watched you struggle with yourself. My guess
(now don't flare up) 's capitulation. Yes?

THOMAS If you're my oldest friend you ought to know
I'd never let myself descend so low.
Still at the breast I started to drink in
chaste principles and pride and discipline.
Think of my Rajput mother who would ride
fearless through danger at the Governor's side.
Think of her merits. She surpassed most men.
Then say 'capitulation'. Think again.
And you know very well you played your part
stamping the Governor's image on my heart.
Your schoolroom stories of my father stirred
my blood to emulate the things I heard,
a giant cannibal fought hand to hand,
the cripplers grappled with, mutilation banned,
dacoits encountered, and suppressed by law,
rebellions put down, and so much more.
Like hunting tigers! All the rest in trees
he goes on foot as coolly as you please,
waits till its almost on him, doesn't shoot,

[4]

but drives a bayonet through the pouncing brute!
All the maneaters that he's bayonetted!
A pyramid of heads! A pyramid!
(pause)
As for that other self, so swift to swear
his plausible empty love-vows everywhere . . .
Oudh! Hyderabad! Kabul! Each of those
stands for some scandal the whole province knows,
scores of 'incidents' throughout Bengal,
O far too many to recall them all —
the purdahs plundered, the zenanas sacked,
many an infamously flagrant act —
the young girl daubed with kohl and henna dye
snatched from a Parsee caravanserai.
The Judge's daughters! Both! The sister's mind,
after her heart was broken, soon declined.
Disowned. A drunkard. Died. And then the other
became the Memsahib and my stepmother!
But she was fortunate in that at least
she had the benefit of rites and priest.
How many times I wanted to cut short
the countless details of that sordid sort.
If only time's recorder could erase
those blots and leave untarnished praise!
Will the gods humiliate me and extort
submission from me of that loathsome sort?
The Governor has exploits he can set
against those foibles and make men forget.
In me, with no such honours, they'd despise
the deliquescence of a lover's sighs.
What trampled monsters give me right to stray
even a little from the narrow way?
And if my pride were, somehow, overcome,
it's not to Lilamani I'd succumb.
Could I be so distracted to dispute
the Governor's veto for forbidden fruit?
She's quite untouchable. A strict taboo
falls like a scimitar between us two.

[5]

Prohibited. The Governor rightly fears
heirs to that family of mutineers.
And so she lives life out, forever barred
from wedlock, and the like, and under guard.
Am I to brave his wrath, espouse her cause,
and show the natives I despise his laws?
BURLEIGH You may protest. I fear it makes no odds
once your fate's been settled by the gods.
And I could see it happening. The more
he tried to blinker you the more you saw.
Hostility fed love. Your father's spite
bathed its victim with an added light.
Love's sweet, so why resist it, so why shy
from feelings common to humanity?
Such stubborn scruple in the face of love
which even your great heroes aren't above!
Siva's avatars subdue sahibs. Few
escape love's clutches. Why should you?
Submit, poor Thomas, pay love your salaams,
yield to the Princess's delightful charms.
The Governor yielded to your mother too
and from their mutual warmth created you.
Without their union you would not be,
you who wrestle against love to struggle free.
So why keep up this pitiful pretence?
Everyone has seen the difference.
For days now, even weeks, you have become —
how should one put it — well, less 'mettlesome'.
Nobody has seen you on 'the morning ride'
racing your ponies by the riverside.
You don't play polo, you no longer train
wild Arab horses to accept the rein.
Your weapons rust. No more the hue and cry
we made the jungle ring with you and I.
Like someone drugged on *bhang*, all heavy-eyed,
sick of some passion that you seek to hide,
it seems so obvious. You're all ablaze,
dazed and bewildered in a lover's maze.

[6]

The little Princess is it? Lost your heart?
THOMAS   I'm going to find my father, and must start.
BURLEIGH I rather think her ladyship expects
          before you go your 'filial' respects!
THOMAS   Present 'the Memsahib' with my salaams.
(exit Thomas Theophilus. enter Ayah)
BURLEIGH Good morning, ayah! Well, no new alarms?
AYAH   The Memsahib! She seems to *want* to die.
          Her days and nights are spent in agony.
          There's nothing I can do. She never sleeps.
          but stares all through the night and sighs and weeps.
          First wants the jalousies wide open, then
          almost at once they must be closed again.
          She wants the punkah fast, the punkah slow,
          too high, she says, to cool her, then too low.
          For hours she gazes at the silver thread
          that marks hot weather, wishing herself dead;
          she points and says: *Ayah, when it reaches there*
          my lungs will have exhausted all the air.
          Now she wants to see the day. It seems
          her brief siestas bring her dreadful dreams.
          She asks, nay, sahib, she commands no eye
          shall gaze upon her in her agony . . .

(exit Burleigh. enter Memsahib)

MEMSAHIB / X no more / X I can't. Must stop.
          No strength! / X Can't move another step.
          Dazzled. My eyes. O ayah, I can't bear
          the sudden brightness. Sun. Light. Glare.
          Can't, ayah, can't bear the light. The heat.
          I don't seem able to stay on my feet.
          aaaggghhh . . .
                              (sits)
AYAH   Heaven hear our desperate prayer.
MEMSAHIB These stifling rags! / X / give me air!
          My hair piled up? Wound round? And who did that
          Cumbered my reason with a lumpish plait?
          It weighs like a stone. What meddling little maid

[7]

burdened my leaden brain with this huge braid?
Aaah all things weary me, and make me vexed!
AYAH   Your wishes change one minute to the next.
Tired of your boudoir, you it was who said;
The sunrise, ayah. Help me out of bed.
You wanted dressing, wanted your hair done —
to be presentable to see the sun.
You said: *Let in the sun, I want to see.*
Now you shrink from it in agony.
MEMSAHIB   That's where it all started, that red fire.
/ X / X blinding, consuming . . . Ayah
its light sinks in, right in, to scrutinise
the sordidness concealed behind my eyes.
This is the last time that I'll have to gaze
on those all-seeing, penetrating rays.
AYAH   O all you ever talk about is dying . . .
MEMSAHIB   The jungle clearing, watching dustclouds flying . . .
horse and boy one animal, the hard sound
of hoofbeats on the baked hot weather ground . . .
nearer . . . nearer . . .
AYAH   Memsahib?
MEMSAHIB   Mad! Oh no . . .
Wandering! Letting reason and desire go.
Your gods, the gods of India possess
my darkened mind and make it powerless.
I can feel my whole face hot with shame
blushing for dreadful things I daren't name.
AYAH   Blush, Memsahib, but blush that you stay mute
and make your sufferings much more acute.
Scorning pity, to all our pleas a stone,
do Memsahibs die loveless and alone?
You're letting yourself die. Three times the night
has dropped its purdah and obscured the light.
without you tasting food. You pine away.
In letting go, Memsahib, you betray
your husband, children, and the source of life.
The Governor Sahib needs his faithful wife!
Think when the children come and you're not here,

[8]

	the Governor away, have you no fear

the Governor away, have you no fear
of what the Rajput woman's son might do
to helpless children out of hate for you.
Your children in Belait, have you no thought
for them being subject to the half-breed's sport?
Thomas Theophilus . . .

MEMSAHIB   God!

AYAH *(triumphant)*   Still feel then?

MEMSAHIB Ayah, never refer to him again.

AYAH If I thought that it would rouse you I'd recite
Thomas Theophilus day and night.
Live, Memsahib, live. Mother love demands.
Live and save your children from his hands.
To let that half-breed Rajput colt control
those who survived you should affront your soul,
that cruel, heartless half-breed who can't feel
grind Sahib's pukka sons beneath his heel?
No time to waste. Each moment of delay
Memsahib's precious lifeblood ebbs away.
While there's an ember left that still glows red,
fan life into flame. Come back from the dead.

MEMSAHIB My guilty life has dragged out far too long.

AYAH Guilt! Guilt! Your guilty life! What guilt? What
                              wrong?
What blood of innocents have those hands spilt?
How could Memsahib's hands be stained with guilt?

MEMSAHIB They're not. My hands are clean enough. You're
                              right.
I would to God my heart were half so white.

AYAH What horror did that heart of hers hatch out
that Memsahib's so pentinent about?

MEMSAHIB Better to let my heart's dark secret go
with my dead body to the earth below.

AYAH Pray do, pray do! But if Memsahib dies
she must find someone else to close her eyes.
Memsahib's life fades fast. Before it fades
her ayah goes down first to warn the shades.
Doors to oblivion are all unbarred.

[9]

One knocks and enters. It is never hard.
When all one's hopes and longings have been
wrecked
despair can guide one to the most direct.
Has ayah's faithfulness once failed the test?
The Memsahib was nursed upon this breast.
I left my little children and my man
far, far behind me in Baluchistan
to care for you. I even held your hand
crossing black water to the Sahib's land.
Daughter of Judge Sahib, will you repay
love and devotion in this cruel way?

MEMSAHIB Don't ayah. Stop insisting. It's no good.
This unspeakable truth would chill your blood.

AYAH Is truth so terrible, Memsahib? *Wai*,
could anything be worse than watch you die?

MEMSAHIB I'll die in any case. With twice the shame
once guilt, that's better nameless, gets a name.

AYAH *(on her knees)*
Memsahib, by these tears that wet your dress
rid ayah of her anguish, and confess.

MEMSAHIB *(after a pause)*
You wish it? Then I will. Up, off your knees.
(pause)

AYAH Memsahib made her promise. Tell me. Please.

MEMSAHIB I don't know what to say. Or how to start.
(pause)

AYAH Tell me, Memsahib. You break my heart.

MEMSAHIB *(sudden vehemence)*
Mother! Driven by the dark gods' spite
beyond the frontiers of appetite.
A *judge's* wife! Obscene! Bestialities
Hindoos might sculpture on a temple frieze!

AYAH Forget! Forget! The great wheel we are on
turns all that horror to oblivion.

MEMSAHIB Sister! Abandoned . . . by him too . . . left
behind . . .
driven to drugs and drink . . . Out of her mind!

[10]

AYAH Memsahib, no. Don't let black despair
flail at your family. Forebear. Forebear.
MEMSAHIB It's India! Your cruel gods athirst
for victims. Me the last and most accursed!
AYAH *(truth dawning)*
Not love?
MEMSAHIB Love. Like fever.
AYAH Memsahib, whom?
MEMSAHIB Witness once more in me my family's doom.
I love . . . I love . . . I love . . . You know the
one
I seemed to hate so much . . . the Rajput's son . . .
AYAH Thomas Theophilus? The half-breed! Shame!
MEMSAHIB I couldn't bring myself to speak his name.
AYAH *Wai*, Memsahib, all my blood congeals.
Love's a running sore that never heals.
Our India destroys white womankind,
sapping the body, softening the mind . . .
MEMSAHIB It's not a sudden thing. This black malaise
struck at the very heart of hopeful days.
My wedding day in fact. The very day
I gave my solemn promise to obey
the Governor Sahib, turning down the aisle,
I glimpsed his son. That steely, distant smile!
I saw him, blushed, then blenched. I couldn't
speak.
Things swam before my eyes. My limbs felt weak.
My body froze, then blazed. I felt flesh scorch
as Siva smoked me out with flaming torch.
I sensed the gods of India were there
behind the throbbing heat and stifling air.
Heart beat like a tom-tom, punkah flapped
backwards and forwards and my strength was
sapped.
I felt you mocking, India, you brewed
strange potions out of lust and lassitude,
dark gods mocking, knowing they can claim
another woman with the Judge's name,

[11]

picking off the family one by one
each destroyed by lust and Eastern sun.
I tried to ward them off. I tried to douse
my heart's fierce holocaust with useless vows.
Tried the *bazaar*! Besought a Hindoo priest
to placate his deities. But nothing ceased.
I saw that sacrifice was offered at the shrine
of every god you Hindoos hold divine —
Siva, Kali, Krishna . . . that shaped stone . . .!
essayed their names myself, but could intone
only young Thomas's. He was my Lord.
He was the deity my lips adored.
His shape pursued me through the shimmering
                                          air.

I tried to flee him. He was everywhere.
O most unspeakable — In Sahib's bed
the son's eyes staring from his father's head!
Against every natural impulse of my soul
I played the stepmother's embittered role,
and had him hounded, and got Thomas sent
back home to Britain into banishment,
forced from his father's arms, his father's heart.
My husband and his favourite prised apart.
At first, relief. I started breathing. With him gone
I put the mask of Governor's Lady on.
I led a wholesome and quite blameless life,
the model mother and submissive wife,
grand lady and efficient chatelaine
adopting public roles to stifle pain.
Useless distractions, purposeless pretence!
The pain, when he returned, was more intense.
The old foe face to face and no escape.
The scars of love's old wounds began to gape,
the old sores fester, the flesh weep blood.
Nothing staunches love or stems the flood.
No longer veins on fire beneath the skin,
ravenous India had her claws deep in.
Ayah, ayah, O I utterly detest

[12]

this cancerous passion that consumes my breast.
I was about to die, and hide away
this sordid secret from the light of day.
But your entreaties wouldn't let me rest.
I gave in to your tears and I confessed.
Save your tears for after. Please don't try
to stir me back to life. I want to die.

(enter Governor's ADC)

ADC Your Ladyship, alas, no one would choose
to bring your Ladyship this bitter news,
but someone had to. It's already known
by almost everyone but you alone.
His Excellency, the Governor of Bengal
is dead. Or killed. His death deprives us all.

(silent agony from Memsahib)

AYAH *Wai!*

ADC I regret there's nothing we can do
to bring him, or his relics, back to you.
The 'son' already knows. The news was brought
by scouts returned from searching to the Fort.

(more silent agony)

Your ladyship, I fear that there is more.
Bazaar talk mentions riot, even war.
Down from the mountains a murderous horde
have put a frontier outpost to the sword.
And Ranjit's daughter under house arrest
may be the focal point for fresh unrest.
There's panic in the quarters. What we need
's your Ladyship herself to give a lead.
Most vital in such times a figurehead,
someone to look to in the Governor's stead,
an example to the others, brave and calm,
someone to salute to and salaam.

(pause)

The Governor's (mm) 'son' 's about to go . . .
Commands a following . . . could overthrow
the rule of law . . . ambition thwarted, rank
from both his strains, own future pretty blank . . .

[13]

nobility on one and on the other
Rajput royal blood from his wild mother,
with disaffection rife he might decide
to throw his lot in with his mother's side.
Some of us consider that it's right
not to let the boy out of our sight.

AYAH The Memsahib has noted your report.
Now allow her time for grief and thought.

(exit ADC)

To think I thought it all a waste of breath
trying to talk Memsahib back from death.
I'd almost given up, prepared to go
with Memsahib to the world below.
His Excellency Sahib is no more.
The bazaar is humming with these threats of war.
His widow must put on the bravest front
for all the sahibs in the cantonment.
Memsahib, live! Fling guilt and shame aside.
Forget this pact with death, this suicide.
The Governor Sahib journeying beyond
releases you from shame and breaks your bond.
Death has condescended to remove
all barriers. Your love's a normal love.
Memsahib need no longer veil
a love which Death has placed within the pale.
It's likely that the half-breed Rajput colt
will swing to the other side and will revolt,
unite with Lilamani and make war
against the Company and rule of law.
Try to persuade him loyalty is best.
Soften the stubbornness within his breast.

MEMSAHIB Very well! Your arguments prevail. I'll try,
if there are means to help me, not to die.
If duty to my kin in this dark hour
can give me back one spark of vital power.

(enter Lilamani with Tara her attendant)

LILAMANI In here? The Governor's son? I don't believe . . .

[14]

To speak with me? With *me!* To take his leave?
Can this be true? Is this happening to me?
TARA   The first of many blessings. You'll soon see.
Those suitors that the cruel tyrant banned
will soon flock unopposed to seek your hand.
Soon, Rani Sahiba, soon your royal due,
freedom and empire will devolve on you.
LILAMANI   I thought it all bazaar talk, but now, no.
I see from your glad face it must be so.
TARA   The brute who loosed the redcoat cannonade
on Rani's noble brothers joins them as a shade.
LILAMANI   So, the Governor is dead. How did he die?
TARA   The most fantastic stories multiply —
much speculation, but one rumour's rife
how, yet again unfaithful to his wife,
he helped another Sahib violate
the Maharani of a native state,
cloaking the nature of his real pursuit,
licentiousness called 'law-enforcement'. Brute!
Some say beyond the frontier, beyond
the forbidden river, Indus, into Khond.
They disappeared (they say in the bazaar)
into the place where ghosts and dead souls are,
the two white sahibs standing without dread
among dark multitudes of silent dead!
LILAMANI   It's not possible! A living man descend
among the ghostly dead before his end.
He must have been bewitched. The evil eye!
TARA   You seem to doubt his death, your Highness, why?
Everyone believes what I have said.
The Governor is dead, your Highness, dead.
The Memsahib, with sahibs from the Fort,
anxious for their skins are holding court,
worriedly debating under swinging fans
potential chaos and contingent plans.
They must be organized before the rain.
LILAMANI   Do you suppose his son is more humane?
Would he look on my plight with more regard?

[15]

TARA   I'm sure he would.

LILAMANI   No. No. He's very hard.
She'd be most foolish the woman who expects
kind treatment from a man who hates our sex.
Haven't you noticed how he'll never ride
anywhere near us but reins aside?
You know what people say about how stern
he is, a piece of ice that will not burn.

TARA   Too much phlegmatic Britain in his veins
dampens the Rajput warmth his blood contains.
I know the *myth*: ascetic, cold, severe,
but not, I've noticed, with your Highness near.
The reputation made me scrutinize
this paragon's cold face and flint-like eyes.
I saw no coldness there. His inmost heart
and what they say of him are poles apart.
He was enslaved the first time both your eyes
exchanged shy glances, and although he tries
in your presence to turn his eyes away,
his eyes stay riveted, and won't obey.
To call him lover would offend his pride
but looks tell everything that mere words hide.

LILAMANI   You've known me all my life, would you have
                                    thought
this shadow puppet of harsh fortune brought
into a world of bitterness and tears
should ever feel such love and its wild fears?
I, last of Ranjit's noble household, forced
to watch my brothers face the holocaust.
My father bayonetted! The redcoat guns
killed my six brothers. All my father's sons.
The eldest, proud and strong, a bloody mess
blown from a cannon into nothingness.
Smoking smithereens! India's red mud
churned even redder with her children's blood.
A state with no new Rajah on the throne.
Only I survive, defenceless and alone,
and drag my life out under strict taboo,

[16]

constant surveillance, what I think, say, do,
everywhere I go the Sahib's spies
watch all my movements with their prying eyes.
What is he afraid of? That love's warm breath
might bring my angry brothers back from death.
As if weak love-pangs such as mine could fan
long burnt out cinders back into a man.
You also were aware I could despise
the wary Sahib and his watchful spies,
indeed, love meant so little to me then
I almost could have thanked the Governor's men
for taking so much trouble to provide
external aids for what I felt inside,
that scorn I had of love. Until my eyes
first saw his son, and I felt otherwise.
It's not the handsomeness and blazoned grace
that Nature's lavished on his form and face
(which he's unconscious of, or quite ignores)
it's not entirely those that are the cause,
but something rarer and more precious still:
his father's good's in him without the ill,
the strengths that earned the Governor his great
name
but not those weaknesses that mar his fame.
And what I love the most, I must confess,
is his obdurate scorn, his stubbornness.
The Memsahib made Governor Sahib fall—
grabbing a heart available to all.
You can't call conquest waiting in the queue
until the 'conquered' one gets round to you.
No sense of victory where many more
have planted standards in the field before.
No, but to triumph over and subdue
a heart subject to no one until you,
to captivate and make a man of steel
know the pangs of love and learn to feel,
to make a man half-gladdened, half-forlorn,
finding himself in chains he's never worn,

[17]

chafing the harness that he half wants on,
fretting for freedom, but half glad it's gone,
that's what I call triumph, that's the kind
of hard-won victory I have in mind,
the uphill struggle it's a thrill to win —
breaking the wild, unwilling stallion in.
Whatever am I thinking though.
He's obstinate. He'd sneer at me I know.
Then perhaps you'll hear my outraged cries
against that haughty pride I eulogize.
That rod of iron bend?

TARA   You soon will know.
He's coming now.

(enter Thomas Theophilus ready to travel)

THOMAS   Madam, before I go
I wanted a few words with you to say
your position might well alter from today.
My father's dead. My presentiment was strong
that fate, not folly kept him gone so long.
No, nothing less than death could overthrow
my noble father, no mere mortal foe.
Only some darker superhuman force
could quench the hero's meteoric course.
My father *was* a hero. Fate sees fit
to take his brilliance and extinguish it.
Acknowledge his great virtues, even you,
and give the good in him its proper due.
Learn from a son's deep love to moderate
your just resentment and your family's hate.
Were I the Governor I'd countermand
the law forbidding men to seek your hand.
If I were on this dais you'd dispose
of self and heart exactly as you chose.
If I were my dead father I'd revoke
his interdictions, lift that cruel yoke . . .

LILAMANI And even that you think of doing so
moves me more deeply than you'll ever know.
The ties of generosity like yours

[18]

	bind me more strictly than your father's laws.
THOMAS	No, let me finish. If I had any say
	you'd be a *reigning* princess. Now. Today.
	Your country gagged on blood. Blood, so much blood
	even the sun-baked earth was turned to mud,
	your brother's bloody gobbets and splashed gore
	splattered like catsup from the cannon's jaw.
	Though I'm ambitious I can never rise
	because of my mixcd blood, my dual ties.
	Though my ambition's balked I can aid yours,
	and, if I may, I'd gladly serve yo'ur cause,
	in the only way I can, behind the scenes —
	the mediator's role, the go-between's!
LILAMANI	Can I believe my ears? Is all this true?
	What friendly deity persuaded you?
	To put your future into jeopardy,
	your precarious existence! All for me!
	It's quite enough to see you moderate
	your hate for me and . . .
THOMAS	Hate you, Madam? Hate!
	So self respect and pride can brand a man
	as some unpacified barbarian?
	Wasn't my mother human just like yours?
	Am I some jungle freak that snarls and roars?
	In any case, by standing at your side,
	the wildest savage would be pacified.
	If anything is magic then you are.
LILAMANI	Sir, I beg you . . .
THOMAS	No, I've gone too far.
	Reason's unseated. Nobody can rein
	runaway passions into line again.
	My confession is so pressing, once begun
	I have no other course but going on.
	Look at this object. Shed tears for its sake,
	watch iron bend, and adamantine break,
	this monument to pride with feet of clay,
	this sun-baked stubbornness that's given way,
	this is the victim, me, who used to scoff

[19]

at lovers bound in chains they can't throw off,
who saw love's storms sink thousands in the sea
and felt secure and said: *this can't touch me,*
now humbled by the lot that most men share
I find myself adrift, I don't know where.
One moment only killed a lifetime's pride.
I submitted to my fate and my will died.
I fled and thrashed about, tried to subdue
the pain that was inside me caused by you.
Shadow, sunlight, dense forest, open space —
it didn't matter where — I saw your face.
I was the hunter once, but now I feel
more like the beast that flinches from the steel.
This prisoner before you vainly tries
to find some shred of self to recognize.
My weapons are beginning to corrode.
I've quite forgotten that I ever rode.
My idle mounts relaxing in their stall
no longer recognize their master's call.
My crudeness must astound you. You'll regret
having this monster snarling in your net.
You should value even more your praises sung
by such a novice and unpractised tongue.

(enter Burleigh)

BURLEIGH Her ladyship desires an interview.
I'm really not sure why.

THOMAS   With me?

BURLEIGH   With you.
I'm not sure of the reason. All I know
's she wishes a few words before you go.

THOMAS How can I face her now, or she face me?

LILAMANI I beg you lay aside your enmity.
She shares in your bereavement. Try to show
a little sympathy before you go.

THOMAS I need some too. From you. Give me some sign
of your reactions to those words of mine.
My offers? Heart? What *am* I to believe?

LILAMANI That I am just as willing to receive

[20]

as you to give. Your gift of love alone
is worth all worldly powers or mere throne.
(exit Lilamani making the gesture of namaste *to Thomas
Theophilus)*

THOMAS *(to Burleigh)*
Soon the sun'll be too high for us to start.
Please tell the men we're ready to depart,
then come back in a breathless hurry, say
how the men are anxious to be on their way.
I could dispense with farewells of this sort.
Friend, I depend on you to cut it short.

(exit Burleigh)
*(enter Memsahib, and Ayah who remains behind the
colonnade)*

MEMSAHIB I'm told, sir, that you're anxious to depart.
I'd hoped to shed the grief that's in my heart
and blend my tears with yours, and to declare
that, with this sense of danger in the air,
now that we know for sure your father's gone,
I scarcely have the will to carry on.
The spirit of unrest extends and grows . . .
I'm expendable to you, though, I suppose.
It wouldn't worry you, stepmother fed
to vultures, dogs . . . I'm sure you wish me dead.

THOMAS I've never wished you anything so bad.

MEMSAHIB I could have understood it if you had.
To all appearances I seemed hell-bent
on causing you much suffering and torment,
stepmother on the warpath, out for blood,
wreaking devastation where she could.
To all appearances! How could you know
the sad reality that lay below?
My schemes and subtle hints had one design
to keep your person far away from mine.
Suffocated by proximity,
stifled by contact of the least degree,
I wanted space between us, and so much
not even the lands we lived in came in touch.

[21]

Only with you in Britain, only then
could I begin to live and breathe again.
If penalties are guaged to the offence
and your hostility's my recompense
for what seemed mine to you, were you aware,
you'd know that punishment was less than fair.
No other woman ever fitted less
the type of stepmother aggressiveness . . .

THOMAS   A mother, Madam, as is too well known
rejects outsiders to protect her own.
It's said to be a not uncommon fate
of second marriages, this kind of hate.

MEMSAHIB   O I must be the one exception then
that proves your rule. Or you must think again.
The feelings of your own stepmother are . . .
rather different . . . different by far . . .

THOMAS   Madam, it's still too early to succumb.
It's still just possible that news may come.
Your grief, perhaps, is somewhat premature.
Somewhere your husband is alive, I'm sure.
My father will come back. His life seems charmed.
India's dark gods won't have him harmed.
I've often thought that Siva and his crew
favoured my father, somehow, haven't you?

MEMSAHIB   There is no voyage home from where he's gone.
No gods that anyone can call upon.
Even the gods of India give way
once greedy Death has fastened on its prey.
What am I saying? Dead? How could he be
when I can see him now in front of me?
I feel my heart . . . Forgive me. My distress
makes me, I fear, too prone to foolishness.

THOMAS   I see that through desire a loving wife
can bring the man she longs for back to life.
As if you see him when you gaze at me!

MEMSAHIB   I pine, sir. Yes. And smoulder. Desperately.
I love your father, anxious to forget
the fickle social butterfly who'd set

[22]

his cap at almost anything in skirts.
That's one side of your father that still hurts.
I see the Governor's womanizing ghost
ravish the consort of his present 'host'!
When I say I love him I don't mean
the womanizer and the libertine,
no, I remember the attentive him,
still diffident, one might say almost, grim,
yet so attractive, fresh, he could disarm
everybody with his youthful charm,
whether they were sahibs or Hindoo.
In all his youthful pride he looked like you,
Your bearing, eyes, the way you sometimes speak,
the same aloofness and the same . . . physique.
(pause)
Mother was 'ill', and outbreaks of bad crime
kept Father on the circuits all the time;
my sister and myself felt lonely, *then*
your famous father swam into our ken.
A wild maneater of prodigious size
began most dreadfully to terrorize
the province that we lived in, and it claimed . . .
O . . . scores of victims, eaten, mauled and
                                       maimed.
A hunter even then of great repute
your father was called in to kill the brute.
He'd taken on so many beasts like these
he seemed like Theseus or like Hercules.
With his adventurous, eccentric life,
his exploits, books, his loves, his Rajput wife,
all this, to us two sisters, made him seem
the complete answer to a young girl's dream.
We fell in love with him right from the start,
two sisters rivals for the same man's heart!
A pity you weren't there, that you weren't one
sent out to help. Too young to hold a gun!
The younger daughter might have been less slow,
less prone to stand back for her sister. No!

[23]

I would have taken the initiative.
Everything she gave, I too would give.
I would have led you to exactly where
the monstrous tiger had its tangled lair.
I would have shown you every little twist
to where the jungle's deep and gloomiest.
I sense your shots sink home with a soft thud!
The stillness of the beast! The smell of blood!
But for a few dim stars, the endless drone
of chirring insects we are quite alone.
Palpable jungle darkness all around.
Would I have cared if we were lost or found?
With you beside me and the night so black
who would ever want the daylight back?

THOMAS   Madam . . . I don't think ever in my life . . .
Have you forgotten you're my father's wife?

MEMSAHIB   Forgotten? I? What leads you to infer
that I no longer value honour, sir?

THOMAS   Forgive me, Madam. I acknowledge to my shame
an unpardonable slander on your name.
I didn't understand . . . I couldn't tell . . .
I think . . . *(turns)*

MEMSAHIB   You understood me very well!
I love you. Love! But when I spell out love
don't think that it's a passion I approve.
Do you suppose I wouldn't if I could
banish this fever throbbing in my blood?
I'm more hateful in my own than in your eyes.
India's chosen me to victimize.
I call on India to testify
how one by one she bled my family dry,
the gods of India whose savage glee
first gluts itself on them and now on me,
my mother and my sister, now my turn
to sizzle on love's spit until I burn.
You know very well how much I tried
to keep my distance, O I tried. I tried.
Keeping my distance led me to devise

[24]

a barrier of hate built up of lies —
I faked hard-heartedness, I cracked the whip,
filled you with hatred for her Ladyship,
was everything they say stepmothers are
until the Memsahib was your *bête noire*.
What use was that? I made you hate me more
only to love you fiercer than before.
I found you even harder to resist —
you were most beautiful when wretchedest.
You'd soon see if you looked at me! I said,
if for a second you could turn your head,
and, just for a moment, look into my eyes.
I think that even you would realize.
Aaggh! Revenge yourself. Go on, chastise
me for foul passions you despise.
There were many monsters that your father slew.
He missed the 'maneater' in front of you.
How did he ever let this vile beast pass?
YOU give this animal the *coup de grace!*
Yes, take the sword he gave you and destroy
the Governor's widow who dare love his boy.
Get your father's sword out. Thrust! Thrust!
                                        Thrust!
Kill the monster while it reeks of lust.
Or if you think that I'm too vile to kill,
and will not strike, give me the sword. I will.
(struggles with him)
                Give me it!
*(enter Ayah emerging from colonnade and snatching the
sword away)*
AYAH   Stop, Memsahib. Come away.
                Think if you're noticed in such disarray.
                Someone's coming. Memsahib! The disgrace!
(exeunt Memsahib and Ayah still carrying the sword)
(enter Burleigh)
BURLEIGH Her Ladyship? Dragged off? My boy, your face!
THOMAS We've got to get away from here. We must.
                I feel such nausea, and such disgust.

[25]

I feel so utterly polluted . . . she . . .
No. Consign the horror to eternity.

BURLEIGH Thomas, the men are ready to depart.
We'd best be off before the troubles start.
Your father's death is felt as the first blow
of widespread insurrection from below.
Some rumours though insist he isn't dead.
Seen somewhere near the frontier. So it's said.

THOMAS Nothing must be ignored. Sift every clue.
Anything we find we'll follow through,
I don't care what the sources of it are —
returning scouts, or spies, or the bazaar.

(exit Burleigh)

But if he's dead, I'll help to bring this land
under a cleaner, less corrupted hand.

(exit Thomas Theophilus)

ACT TWO

(Bugle-calls off-stage. Enter Chuprassie and Servants. enter ADC. enter Memsahib and Ayah)

MEMSAHIB Tell the Chuprassie, please, the answer's NO.
The Memsahib's not fit to go on show.

(exit ADC ushering Chuprassie and Servants out)

Hide me from the world's what they should do,
conceal my raw desire from public view.
Such thoughts which never ought to even reach
the conscious mind I've put into plain speech.
And how he heard it all, that block of wood,
making as if he hadn't understood!
I pour out my secret, inmost heart
and all he wants to do is to depart!
He pawed the ground, and had no other thought
than how he could best cut my ravings short.
The way he stood and shuffled with bowed head
could only make my shame a deeper red.
And even when I had his swordblade pressed

[26]

all ready to be plunged into my breast,
did he snatch it back? Made no attempt!
Just stared at me! Such coldness! Such contempt!
I touch it once, that's all, and in his sight
it's been polluted by some dreadful blight.

AYAH Self-pity, Memsahib, the way you brood
nourish a passion that is best subdued.
What would the Judge Sahib your father say
if he were still alive and here today?
He'd say: Find peace in duty, daughter, find
some public service to assuage your mind.
Duties a Governor's widow can perform
to help the Sahibs ride the coming storm.

MEMSAHIB The storm's already raging in my soul.
The Memsahib's no touchstone of control!
My reason's a torn punkah that can't move
the airless atmosphere of febrile love.
O reason soon seems sapped and comatose
shut up in passions so stifling and close!

AYAH You could go home.

MEMSAHIB   And leave him here? O no!

AYAH You had him sent away.

MEMSAHIB   Yes, years ago.
It's too late now. He knows. He knows. I've crossed
the frontier of virtue and I'm lost.
Hope, for a moment, caught me unawares
and all my shame was bared to his cold stares.
When I was quite prepared for my demise
you dangled life and love before my eyes.
All your native guile and honied speech
put the unattainable within my reach.
I wanted, *wanted* O so much to die.
You had to come and stop me. Why? Why? Why?

AYAH Innocent or guilty, Memsahib, I'd do
even more than that if it's for you.
Spare your ayah though. Can you forget
that face of his, indifferent and hard-set?

MEMSAHIB Perhaps it's innocence and virgin youth

[27]

that makes his ways seem clumsy and uncouth.
Look at the stations where he's had to live
among the most far-flung and primitive.
Let's try to understand. Perhaps that's why.
It's the novelty of love that makes him shy.
So perhaps we shouldn't condemn him yet.

AYAH His Rajput blood, Memsahib, don't forget.
His mother was barbarian, half-wild.

MEMSAHIB Half-wild or not, she loved. She bore this child.

AYAH He hates all women and would never yield.

MEMSAHIB Good, his hostility helps clear the field.
If love is something that he'll never feel
let's search elsewhere for his Achilles heel.
Ambition! Dual parentage frustrates
all hopes he might have had in both his states.

(listens)

Listen! Horses! Go make the boy believe
in greatness I could help him to achieve.
Say how my father's name would help provide
some useful access on the legal side.
O tell him now the Memsahib has schemes
by which he'll realize his inmost dreams.
Ayah, anything! Urge, implore him, cry.
Say the Memsahib's about to die.
And if it seems that you must grovel, do.
Do anything. My life depends on you.
Anything!

(exit Ayah)

          India, you see it all
watching the haughty stoop, the mighty fall.
Your gods possess dark powers no man can flout.
How much more blood of mine can you squeeze out?
How much further down can I be brought?
If you want more, you'll find much better sport
hunting a quarry harder to destroy,
fleeter of foot, a virgin. Hunt the boy!
O India! There's much more good pursuit
chasing the suppler, more elusive brute.

[28]

It's your sensual nature he ignores.
Avenge yourself. We have a common cause:
to make him love . . .

(enter Ayah)

So soon? The answer's no.
He wouldn't listen even. Let him go.

AYAH Silence those feelings. Never let them stir.
Remember your old self and who you were.
Banish such thoughts for ever from your head.
Your husband, Governor Sahib, isn't dead.
The people cheer, those few who recognize
the Governor Sahib in his new disguise.
Any moment now he will appear.

MEMSAHIB The Governor! Alive? And almost here!
If he's alive, all I can do is die.

AYAH Again you talk of death, Memsahib. Why?

MEMSAHIB And had I died this morning as I planned
and not let your persuasion stay my hand,
I might have earned some tears, and saved my face.
All I deserve's dishonour. Death. Disgrace.

AYAH Death! Death!

MEMSAHIB What have I done? What have I done?
The Governor will be here, and with his son.
The one who saw her grovel with cold eyes
will watch her Ladyship resort to lies,
tears of frustration just shed for the boy
turned so deceitfully to wifely joy,
the wife still burning for her husband's son
go through the motions of reunion,
the still flushed consort desperate to convince
the husband she betrayed not minutes since.
There's just a chance that he's so overcome,
so anxious for his father, he'll stay dumb.
Or maybe he'll tell all through sheer disgust
at seeing his father's wife display her lust.
And if he does keep quiet, I'm not one
to shirk the consequences of what I've done.
I can't forget things. I'm not one of those

[29]

frequenters of mess balls and evening shows,
who can commit their crimes and uncontrite
are never troubled by a sleepless night.
My conscience hurts me. Hurts. Each word I said
keeps echoing and booming through my head.
Those beastly heads his study's full of roar
as we enter *adulteress* and *whore.*
I see the hand of judgement start to scrawl
graffiti of my guilt on every wall.
Death's the only answer. Death. A swift release
from pain. For me and for my conscience, peace.
Is it so much to die? To one who's racked
by great torment it's a very simple act.
The only fear that lingers in my mind
is for my children. The shame I leave behind.
So many generations of blood-pride
obliterated by my suicide.
Think of the children, orphans, forced to face
those stories (all too true) of my disgrace.

AYAH I do. I weep for them. They'll suffer hell.
I fear those things will happen you foretell.
But why, Memsahib, why must you expose
your little children to such ills as those.
If you die, all that's likely to be said
's she couldn't face her husband, so she fled.
What greater sign of guilt could you provide
than plunging headlong into suicide.
Memsahib, think! This suicide of yours
does more than lawyers to defend his cause.
Your death saves him. Your tragedy becomes
a camp-fire story for his hunting chums.
Without you here, there's no more can be done.
I'm a poor ayah. He's the Governor's son.
My word against his son's! Huh, take my part
against a cherished favourite of his heart!
Then all India will hear and quite ignore
in all the din against the one voice for.
Memsahib I would rather die with you

[30]

than live to hear such stories, false or true.
Thomas Theophilus, Memsahib? How
do you feel about the half-breed now?

MEMSAHIB His head should be mounted along with all
the monsters on the Sahib's study wall.

AYAH Then don't give in submissively. Don't lose
without a struggle, Memsahib, accuse
the boy before the boy accuses you.
Who will contradict you if you do?

(takes up sword)

And this, Memsahib, look. Here's evidence:
the weapon in your hands, you, shaken, tense.

MEMSAHIB Purity put down? Innocence oppressed?

AYAH Only keep silent and I'll do the rest.
I suffer fear as well. I feel remorse.
I'd rather die but see no other course.
What are one poor ayah's scruples worth
with her Memsahib buried in the earth?
I'll speak, but making sure his anger goes
only to bitter words and not to blows.
And just supposing guiltless blood were spilt
to save your honour and to spare you guilt,
aren't these the measures that we have to take
when it's a question of your name at stake?
Honour must be saved at all expense
even the sacrifice of innocence.

*(enter Chuprassie and servants. The Governor pushes
through them and enters disguised as an Indian)*

GOVERNOR Fortune relenting has turned foul to fair
and returned me to your arms . . .

MEMSAHIB   Sir, stay there!
Don't desecrate your joy. I've lost all right
to claim the eagerness of your delight.
You have been wronged. Fate brings you from the
                                                        dead
but spits its venom at your wife instead.
No longer fit to bear the name of wife!

(Memsahib hurries off closely followed by Ayah)

[31]

GOVERNOR And this my welcome! The dead brought back to
life.

THOMAS Your wife's the one to question. Only she
can help you clarify this mystery.
If desperation moves you, father, then
heed that of this most desperate of men,
and permit your shaken son to live his life
in some locality not near your wife.

GOVERNOR What? Leave?

THOMAS As long as you, sir, were away,
I'd no alternative except to stay,
protecting those entrusted to my care,
against my will: your wife; and Ranjit's heir.
I did my best, but now with your return
I need no longer stay, sir, and I yearn
to prove myself your son and blood my spear
on prey far grander than wild boar or deer.
By my age, single-handed and alone,
you'd toppled a cruel Sultan from his throne,
shot scores of grim maneaters dead, and quelled
banditry in savage districts, held
the passes against unpacified Afghans
and made the highroads safe for caravans.
How many villagers you went to save
from dacoits or maneaters came to wave
and shout: *Jai! Sirkar ki jai!* around your tent
Glory and victory to the Government!
So many trophies on your walls by then
to satisfy the lifetimes of most men.
Old heroes could retire because they knew
the rule of reason was secure with you.
Obscurity! The undistinguished son
of such a father, and with nothing done!
Even my mother did more things than me.
Father, I feel trapped in this obscurity.
Let me have your weapons. I'll pursue
the fiercest monsters as you used to do.
I'll have the Residency walls and floors

[32]

covered with trophies just as wild as yours.
From private bedroom to official throne
carpetted with beasts I've overthrown.
Or make my going such a noble one
the world would know at last that I'm your son.

GOVERNOR What's this? What contagion of insanity
makes my (so-called) loved ones flee from me?
Why did I ever come back from the dead
to find my family so filled with dread?
Of me? Myself the object to strike fear
into the ones I trusted and held dear!
(*pause*)
O India got into us somehow!
Absolute madness when I look back now,
part imbecility, part foolish prank
and probably the simpkin that we drank,
well anyhow, the upshot of it all
was a midnight entry, via the palace wall,
into a harem. My colleague, ADC
in charge of the suppression of Thuggee,
(he's more hot-blooded than you'd think, that man)
forced the favourite of the local Khan.
And, put it down to India, I'm afraid
that I 'assisted' in his escapade.
Taken by surprise, no time to draw
the tyrant had us seized and bound . . . I saw . . .
He kept . . . God knows what the monsters were.
I tell you even I was frightened, sir.
He kept . . . these somethings hungry in a pit.
I heard my friend thrown screaming into it.
My captor was a beast, obscene, perverse,
given to practises I won't rehearse,
to crude carnalties that overrode
every natural law and human code.
He'd draw the line at nothing. No taboo
would stop him doing what he wanted to.
I was shut up in a hole, a living tomb
so dark it seemed like Hell's own ante-room.

[33]

Chained naked like a beast — six months in there,
barely a spark of light or breath of air!
Then India relented, I suppose.
I broke the sentry's neck and stole his clothes
and made a quick escape, but not before
your father settled his outstanding score
with that black tyrant who'd devised all this.
I dropped him piecemeal down his own abyss,
that devilish despot and foul debauchee
chewed by his pet, flesh-starved monstrosity.
Disguised, I left that hell-hole far behind
restored to light and air, and my right mind.
Anxious to resume my shaken hold
on normal life I find the world turned cold.
This is my hearth and home and surely where
I have some right to breathe a cleaner air.
A season spent in hell, I've no desire
for whiffs of brimstone from the household fire.
I still smell prisons, yet I'm among
the very ones I yearned for for so long.
I see my dear ones with averted face
shunning the welcome of my warm embrace,
my presence striking terror in their soul
and wish I were still shut up in that hole.
I want the truth from you. I want it now.
What wrong has my wife suffered. When? Who?
             How?
Why isn't the culprit under lock and key?
You're in it too! Why don't you answer me?
Speak, why can't you? My flesh and blood! My son!
Is everyone against me? Everyone?
Ah India, I've given you my life.
Deliver up the man who's harmed my wife.
I'll get to know, by fair means or by foul,
what manner of strange monster's on the prowl.
(exit Governor)
 THOMAS O this unventilated atmosphere!
       Burleigh, my blood runs cold with sudden fear.

[34]

What if her Ladyship while still a prey
to her strange frenzy gives herself away?
Instead of a warm son and welcoming wife
my father finds a foul infection rife,
some plague that makes his hearth and home
                                        unclean;
like victims sickening in quarantine,
the wife and son to whom he's been restored,
shivering with symptoms in this fever ward.
As in the jungle when the beaters' ring
closes round the beast that's panicking,
I feel that sense of menace and my heart
thumps as the undergrowth is forced apart.

(enter Ayah displaying the sword of Thomas Theophilus,
and followed by the Governor)

GOVERNOR ANIMAL! / X Now it all comes out!
The reversal everybody spoke about!
The lower self comes creeping up from its lair
out of the dismal swamps of God-knows-where.
It lumbers leering from primeval slime
where it's been lurking, biding it own time.
How could his kind absorb our discipline,
our laws of self-control, our claims of kin.
I've expected far too much. It's in his blood.
Control himself? I don't suppose he could.
One should have known the worst. One ought to
                                        know
that India once hooked in just won't let go.

(he takes the sword)

And this the weapon! One he couldn't lift
when I first gave it him. His father's gift!
I don't suppose his sort acknowledge sin.
Don't blood-ties count? To violate one's kin!
And the Memsahib? Why did she allow
this animal at liberty till now.
Her silence makes his foulness almost fair.

AYAH It was the Sahib's grief she wished to spare.
The Memsahib, so sickened with sheer shame

[35]

was she at kindling his lustful flame,
her desperate feelings turned to suicide,
and but for me, Sahib, she would have died.
I saved her, Sahib. I preserved your wife
in the very act of taking her own life.
In pity for her sorrow and your fears
I now explain the meaning of her tears.

(The Governor drives the sword into the dais on which throne stands)

GOVERNOR Barbarian! No wonder that in spite
of all his efforts I could sense his fright.
His chilly welcome took me by surprise,
felt frozen by the scared look in his eyes.
When did my son first show himself so foul?
When did this animal first start to prowl?

AYAH At the beginning of your married life
the boy already had disturbed your wife.

GOVERNOR And in my absence things came to a head?

AYAH Everything occurred as I have said.
We must not leave her on her own too long.
Allow me to return where I belong.

(exit Ayah)

GOVERNOR *(seeing Thomas enter)*
Good God! Wouldn't anyone be taken in
by looks so seemingly devoid of sin?
No mark of his lascivious offence
sullies that subtle mask of innocence
A beast in human shape! I'd like to brand
ANIMAL on his flank with my own hand!

THOMAS May not a sympathetic son be told
what makes his father's look seem hard and cold?

GOVERNOR After dishonouring your father's name,
still reeking of your lust and smirched with shame,
the animal still has the brazen face
to stand before his father in this place!
Instead of running far away from me
back to the jungle and its savagery,
beyond our influence and rigid laws

[36]

back to the world of bestial lusts like yours.
Unless you want to share the fate of those
whose lawlessness I crushed with iron blows,
unless you want the Governor to show
his famous skill in killing monsters, GO!
India! Remember how I cleared
your countryside of monsters that all feared.
Now in return I ask your gods to take
swift vengeance on this monster for my sake.
If you cherish me in your dark heart,
India, tear this animal apart!

THOMAS Her Ladyship brands me with that foul sin?
it's too revolting even to take in.

GOVERNOR I think I can see through your little game.
Your lust kept secret through the lady's shame.
You loathsome animal, you put your trust
in her reticence to conceal your lust,
That's not enough. You should have had the sense
not to have left behind this evidence,

(taking sword and displaying it to Thomas Theophilus)
or been more systematic, and instead
of leaving her just speechless, left her dead.

THOMAS Why do I stand and hear so black a lie
and not speak truths I'd be acquitted by?
Sir, there are dreadful things I could disclose
nearer to yourself than you suppose.
I could blurt secrets out. I could . . . but no,
give me some credit for not doing so.
I cannot wish more agony on you
but please consider what I am and who.

(Thomas Theophilus takes sword from Governor)
A man first breaks small laws, then treads taboos
basic to all men beneath his shoes.
Like virtue vice develops. It takes time
for petty to turn into heinous crime.
Impossible! The twinkling of an eye
turn innocence to bestiality!
My mother's chastity was her renown.

[37]

That and her courage. I've never let her down.
I made restraint a virtue and subdued
mutinous passions into servitude.
My shibboleths were bridle, curb and bit.
Lust! Bestality! I mastered it!
I'm the one who took restraint so far
that I'm a laughing stock in the bazaar.
You know the soubriquets they call me by,
good-natured, and obscene, as well as I.
I never thought of women, now I'm faced
with charges of black lust. I'm chaste, sir. Chaste!

GOVERNOR Your foul obsession must have taken hold
from very early on to make you cold
to every female influence but one.
Wouldn't some black concubine have done?

THOMAS Father! Sir! It's too much to conceal,
I have to tell the truth. My heart *can* feel.
It feels a chaste emotion, but for one
you yourself placed interdictions on.
It's Lilamani. Under house arrest.
She's stormed my stubborn heart. There, I've
                            confessed.
Despite myself I contravened your law
and this is what I need forgiveness for.

GOVERNOR / X Clever! You're ready to confess
to that to hide the worse lasciviousness!

THOMAS For six months now no matter how I've tried
I've loved. I've loved her, and I'm terrified,
and came to see you now to tell you so.
Sir, how much further do I have to go.
I swear by . . .

GOVERNOR   O the guilty always flee
as a desperate resort to perjury.
Enough! Enough! No more tedious harangues,
if it's on stuff like this your story hangs.

THOMAS You think my story's false, and full of lies?
Your wife, sir, in her heart knows otherwise.

GOVERNOR Animal! How dare you. Don't say any more.

[38]

THOMAS   I'm to be sent away? Where? And how long for?
GOVERNOR   Across the Indus, the 'forbidden river',
             and beyond our frontiers. For ever!
THOMAS   Charged with such crimes, and your curse on my
                                                    head,
             who will welcome me, or give me bread?
GOVERNOR   Peoples exist without *our* discipline,
             the lesser breeds, perhaps they'll take you in.
             Hospitality in the far North West.
             means laying down your wife for any guest.
             You should feel welcome there. I'm sure you'll find
             depraved men, debauchees, of your own kind!
THOMAS   Debauchery! Compare my mother's, my own life
             with that of the woman who conceived your wife.
             Think of my parentage, then hers, and choose.
             Decide whose blood is coming out, sir. Whose?
             Think of my mother, Father! Think! At least
             she wasn't serviced by a slavering beast!
GOVERNOR   Go! Get out of my sight. Or else I'll shout
             for the sentries and have you frog-marched out.
(exit Thomas Theophilus)
             Like shivering and chill preceding fever
             I sense the presence of avenging Siva.
             My spine's an icicle, my inwards knot
             with pity for this monster I begot.
             God, I feel stifled by my wretchedness!
             How did I come to sire a beast like this?
(enter Memsahib)
MEMSAHIB   Your shouting could be heard through all the
                                                    doors.
             It made me terrified to hear those roars
             and bull-like bellowing. I feared far worse
             might follow on your homicidal curse.
             You still have time to call him back. You could.
             O do, I beg you. He's your flesh and blood.
             Spare some thought for me. How could I survive
             knowing that, but for me, he'd be alive.
             Could I live with the knowledge I'm the one

[39]

who turned a father's hand against his son?

GOVERNOR No, not a father's hand. A darker force
than any man's ensures death takes its course.
India owes me some destruction.

MEMSAHIB   No!

GOVERNOR Her gods are swift in paying what they owe.
And now, in all its blackness, tell me all
before the mercury of anger starts to fall.
I want each little detail.

*(The Governor turns and walks to the colonnade. A pause
in which it seems the Memsahib has the truth all ready to
disclose)*

                                        You've not heard
half of the guilt your stepson has incurred.
He launched into a great frenzy against you.
Implied that all you'd said just wasn't true!
And in his own defence he swore that . . . Guess!
He swore he loved the Indian princess!
Lilamani . . .

MEMSAHIB   Swore? What?

GOVERNOR   Tried to confuse
the issue. Lies all lies. A desperate ruse.
(suddenly tense)
I hope whatever happens happens soon.
(leaving)
Then everything washed clean by the monsoon!
(exit Governor)

MEMSAHIB And just when I was coming to his aid!
This thunderclap! This stunning cannonade!
Stung by remorse and guilt I flung aside
my ayah's arms and left her terrified.
O God knows just how far I might have gone
if I'd have let repentance drive me on.
If he hadn't cut me short . . . God knows
I had the truth all ready to disclose.
And Lilamani (*Lilamani!*) stealing
the little boy from me who has no feeling.
The one who'd walled himself completely in

[40]

against invasions of the feminine!
Perhaps his heart's accessible to all.
and he has hundreds at his beck and call.
Women pawing at him from each side
and I'm the only one he can't abide.
The charms of any native concubine
are no doubt more agreeable than mine.
The only one to whom he *can* say no!
Too old, too white for his seraglio!
Chastity? Surfeit! And I'd come to claim
his innocence, and ruin my own name!

(enter Ayah)

Ayah, have you heard the latest? Guess!

AYAH Memsahib, ayah comes to you in real distress.
I wondered why you'd torn yourself away.
I was very much afraid what you might say.

MEMSAHIB Ayah, there's competition. And, guess who?

AYAH Memsahi . . .

MEMSAHIB   He loves another. Yes, it's true.
This fierce quarry no one could hunt down,
who countered blandishments with a cold frown,
this tiger frightening to stand beside,
gentle as a lamb, quite pacified.
That princess . . .

AYAH   Her?

MEMSAHIB   Yes *her*. Agh how much
                                                              more
persecution has India in store?
As if being torn apart by two extremes,
first shivering despair, then fevered dreams,
as if the final insult of his cold rebuff
and all my sufferings were not enough.
Lovers? Them! What native sorcery has thrown
this smokescreen round them? When were they
                                                              alone?
How? When? Where? You knew all along. You
                                                              knew.
You could have told me sooner couldn't you?

[41]

Exchanging glances. Talking. Furtiveness.
Where did they hide, hm? In the forest, yes.
To follow one's feelings through nature's course
without recriminations and remorse,
not to feel criminal, and meet as though
the sun shone on one's love and watched it grow!
Ah! Every day they must wake up and see
vistas with no black clouds, and feel so free!

AYAH   They'll never meet again, Memsahib. Never!
Their love . . .

MEMSAHIB   will survive for ever and ever.
Though they were twenty thousand miles apart
heart would heliograph to exiled heart,
across the Himalayas if need be.
Nothing can come between them. Even me!
Kisses! Promises! Touching one another!
scorning the fury of the mad step-mother.
Their happiness feeds off my jealousy.
That green-eyed monster is destroying me.
That mutinous family! No reason why
the Governor should show her leniency!
The father bayonetted, the brother shot
from a cannon. She should die too. Why not?
She's of their blood. They died. Why should she
                                    live?
Her crime is even harder to forgive.
How smoothly one progresses from the first
tentative transgressions to the worst.
My first steps taken, sick with vertigo,
I inched towards dishonour, now I go
with eyes wide open and with one bold stride
into the black abyss of homicide.
O, those white hands, remember? If I could
I'd plunge them elbow deep in guiltless blood.
How can I bear to have the sun's light pry
through every cranny at my misery?
There's nowhere, nowhere dark enough to hide.
No, everywhere the sun can get inside.

[42]

Close the shutters and black out the glare
you feel it then as heat, and everywhere:
the mercury a hundred in the shade,
the grass screens sprayed with water, and resprayed,
the hopeless, winnowing thermantidote —
heat like some animal that claws one's throat.
There's no escape from that all-seeing eye,
that presence everywhere except to die.
My Hell is India, always at high noon,
with no relief of night, and no monsoon,
and under that red sun's remorseless stare
mankind's grossest secrets are laid bare.
My Hell is such exposure, being brought
a guilty prisoner to my father's court.
I see the Judge's phantom with shocked face
jib at the details of his daughters's case,
hearing his once loved flesh and blood confess
to crimes of monumental loathsomeness.
Aghast but relentless he applies the Law
to horrors even he's not heard before.
His task is Judgement. Judges give no quarter,
and merciless he sentences his daughter.
Father, forgive me. Please forgive me. Try.
Harsh India's destroyed your family.
The same gods in your daughter. Recognize
the lust they kindled blazing in her eyes.
Repentence never lets up its pursuit.
I've broken laws, but never reaped the fruit!
Harried by ill luck till my last breath
all that seems left me is a dreadful death.

AYAH You are in love. And that's your destiny.
You're in the power of some evil eye.
Is love unheard of, even in these parts?
Memsahib, millions have human hearts.
Are you the first or last of us to fall.
Memsahib, love is common to us all.
Weakness is human, Memsahib, submit
to your humanity. Give way to it.

[43]

                    Even the gods, we Hindoos say, who fright
                    mere mortals sometimes, know delight.
                    Not only men, Memsahib, gods above
                    partake of pleasures and the joys of love.
MEMSAHIB   You reptile! Spitting still! The snake still tries
                    to poison the Memsahib with black lies.
                    Your evil whispers drugged my sense of right.
                    The boy I shunned you urged into my sight.
                    Who gave you leave? Who gave you orders? Why
                    did you have to brand him? Now he'll die. He'll die.
                    His father mouths strange curses and implores
                    vengeance and justice from those gods of yours.
                    Let what agonies you've earned spell out the fate
                    of those low persons who corrupt the great.
                    You take our weaknesses and give them scope
                    and grease the incline of the downward slope.
                    Her Ladyship debased, demeaned, brought low,
                    down to the level of your blackness. Go!

*(exit Ayah. Memsahib is left alone with the sense of India
closing in. Exit Memsahib)*
(enter Lilamani, followed by Thomas Theophilus)
LILAMANI   No! No! Your keeping silent's suicide!
                    This sacrifice you make to spare his pride
                    in normal circumstances would be one
                    that's most becoming in a loyal son,
                    but now with danger like a dangling sword
                    it's more a luxury you can't afford.
                    If, without much thought for me, you can consent
                    and so submissively to banishment,
                    then go; leave me to languish and to grieve.
                    But at least defend yourself before you leave,
                    Defend your honour. There's still time yet
                    to persuade your father to retract his threat.
                    If you keep silent then the scales will tip
                    wholly in favour of her Ladyship.
                    Tell everything . . .
THOMAS   Tell everything and show
                    my father his own shame, I couldn't, no.

[44]

Could I bear exposing his wife's lust
and watch his whole life crumble into dust?
The fullest horror's known to only you
and those who witness all we say and do.
If I didn't love you would I have revealed
obscenities to *you* I'd want concealed
even from myself! You gave your word
never to pass on what you have heard.
And even if it proves at my expense
I have to make you swear to reticence.
That gesture of respect for him at least.
From every other tie I feel released.
Remember too that right is on our side.
Sooner or later I'll be justified.
Her Ladyship will surely not elude
the consequences of gross turpitude.
Leave this prison, and its poisoned air,
and follow me to exile, if you dare.
I can offer you the means you need to flee.
Even the guards on watch are all with me.
We could count on powerful allies in our fight
to win you back your throne, your lawful right.
My mother's tribe, the warlike Rajput clan
have sworn allegiance to us to a man.
Mountain chieftains and the Rajah's court
send secret guarantees of their support.
The Memsahib! Why should such as she
prosper by destroying you and me?
Now's the time. Everything is on our side.
And yet you look afraid and can't decide.
LILAMANI There's no dishonour in escape, indeed
I feel it only right I should be freed.
My family's heroes struggled to set free
our subdued people from white tyranny.
Your father is a tyrant and I owe
him no obedience. I'm free to go.
But I'm of royal blood, and many wait
for me to reassume the reins of state,

[45]

the last upholder of my father's name.
My followers permit no hint of shame . . .

THOMAS Nor I! My mother's gods are yours. Suppose
we swear our loyalty in front of those?
Near where my royal mother's buried, she
and all her ancient Rajput family,
there stands a shrine, a very holy place
where no perjurer dare show his face.
To stand in for our fathers we'll invoke
the gods whose shrine it is to join our yoke.

LILAMANI *(seeing Chuprassie enter with three servants)*
The Governor's Chuprassie! Go, please, go.
I'll stay a while so nobody will know.
Send someone I can trust to be my guide
to lead me to the shrine to be your bride.

(she makes the gesture of namaste *to Thomas Theophilus
who, after a pause, returns the gesture and exits.)*
(enter Governor who first confers with Chuprassie)

GOVERNOR I'm told my son's been taking leave of you?

LILAMANI We said farewell. Your 'intelligence' is true!

GOVERNOR Those lovely eyes! It's their work, then, all this?
First to hypnotize that stubbornness!

LILAMANI The truth is something that I can't deny.
He doesn't seem to share your enmity.
He's never treated me like a pariah.

GOVERNOR It doesn't operate like that, desire.
I suppose he swore his love 'for ever more'.
You're not the first. He's said it all before.

(Lilamani remains silent)

You should have kept him on a tighter rein.
Doesn't the competition cause you pain?

LILAMANI It should pain you to vilify your son,
especially so pure and chaste a one.
Have you so little knowledge of his heart?
Can't you tell innocence and guilt apart?
Don't listen to that snake, Memsahib's nurse.
Take back, Sahib, your rash assassin's curse.
Our gods may well give ear to your wild wish

[46]

because they find you brutish, devilish.
Sometimes it's anger makes the gods say yes
and gifts may be the gods' vindictiveness.

GOVERNOR You're trying to throw dust into my eyes.
Love's blinkered you to his depravities.

LILAMANI Take care, Sahib. Your manly strength and
                                                 skills
have notched up many monsters in your kills.
Their glazed eyes watch us talking, but not all
have their heads hung on your study wall.
Your great collection is still missing one . . .
But I'm forbidden to go further by your son.
Strangely enough his love for you's not gone
and his respect prevents my going on.
Unless I leave your presence I'll forget
myself and say things that we'll both regret.

(exit Lilamani. The sound of thunder)

GOVERNOR They're both in league to throw me off the track.
A conspiracy to stretch me on the rack.
In spite of my resolve some doubt still gnaws.
A still small voice cries mercy, and I pause.
Deep in my hardened heart to my surprise
pity still sends out its feeble cries.

(resolved again)
I want it all made absolutely clear.

(shouts)
Chuprassie!

CHUPRASSIE   Sir!

GOVERNOR   Memsahib's ayah. Here.

(exit Chuprassie)
(enter ADC)

ADC Sir! Her Ladyship! Something's very wrong.
She's gripped by God knows what and can't last
                                       long.
Whatever thoughts are passing through her head,
she seems, your Excellency, almost dead.
Her face is ghastly pale, her bloodless lips
seem more a corpse's than her Ladyship's.

[47]

The ayah's been sent packing by your wife.
Fled to the forest careless of her life.
Went to earth where none would give pursuit,
a region best relinquished to the brute.
No blacks and none of us (but you)'d give chase
into that swampy beast-infested place.
The jungle swallowed her. No search would find
much more than shreds of sari left behind.
What drove the woman there nobody knows.

GOVERNOR What's this?

ADC   Her Ladyship finds no repose.
She hugs the children's likenesses, which seems
to calm her for a while, but then she screams
and pushes them away as if she could
no longer bear the thought of motherhood.
She walks or rather lurches to and fro,
not knowing where to sit or where to go.
She looks at one but seems to stare right through.
She knows there's someone there, she's not sure
who.
She sat down at her desk three times and wrote
but each time changed her mind and burnt the note.
For pity's sake, sir, go and see your wife.

GOVERNOR The ayah dead! My dear one sick of life.
Someone fetch my son. I'll hear his case.
Let him defend himself before my face.

*(exit ADC. The Governor listens to the distant thunder of
the coming monsoon)*
O God what if the thing's already done?

(thunder/wind blows through the room. Enter Burleigh)
Ah! Burleigh, you. What's happened to my son?
You've been his tutor how long now? Well nigh . . .
But what's this, man? My God, you're weeping.
Why?

My son! What's happened?

BURLEIGH   *Now* you demonstrate
anxiety on his behalf. It's all too late.
He's dead.

[48]

GOVERNOR	No!
BURLEIGH	The gentlest boy I knew!

And, if I may say so, the most guiltless too.

GOVERNOR My son dead? No! The moment I extend
my arms to him, THEY hound him to his end.

BURLEIGH We moved like a slow cortège out of the town.
Even the horses jogged with heads hung down.
He rode his finest white Arabian steed
at little more than normal walking speed.
The sepoy escort all looked just as grim
and sullen out of sympathy for him.
We're hated, but obeyed because we're feared.
He was almost one of them; admired; revered.
Then from the jungle came a dreadful cry.
Birds and old dry leaves began to fly.
And dust, like blood turned into powder, floats
in huge spirals, blinds us, scours our throats.
The wind got up, increased. The jungle trees
first lent a little to a light stray breeze
then began bending violently and then
just as suddenly sprang straight again;
then bent with force that made the palm leaves
                                          crack.
Then all of a sudden all the sky went black,
and from the deepest darkest part a cry
like the first but lower rent the sky.
Our hearts stand still. Blood freezes in our veins.
Hair stiffens on our frightened horses' manes.
The forest begins heaving like the sea,
and seems to open up, and, suddenly,
we see, festooned with seared lianas, IT
some horrifying, monstrous, composite,
like one of those concoctions that one sees
in dark recesses on a temple frieze.
An old woman told the sepoys it was Siva
in his avatar of monster. They believe her.
You know how sceptical I am, but there
is the monster, and its bellows fill the air.

[49]

The whole earth shudders as it moves its feet
and shambles forward through the shimmering
                        heat.

An epidemic smell, the beast exhales
a stink like cholera from its gold scales.
Then everyone starts running, everyone
except, that is, your son, your fearless son.
We all take shelter in a shrine nearby.
He reins in his horse and does not fly.
We see him all alone, without a fear,
grab that ordinary, native spear
he sometimes went hog-hunting with, and fling
the weapon with sure aim into the thing.
It gushes blood, breathes fire and smoky heat,
squirms and writhes before the horses' feet.
The thing with wide jaws like an open sluice
disgorges gore and vomits blackish juice.
The horses panic. A regular stampede!
He calls out to his own. They take no heed.
The one he's riding bolts and all in vain
he shouts *whoa, whoa,* and tugs hard on the rein.
He wastes his strength. From each champed bit
flies froth and slaver and blood-red spit.
The sepoys say that maddened Siva sank
a sharpened trident into each scorched flank.
They gallop, riderless but one, towards the rocks —
the snap of broken bones and cracked fetlocks,
as they collide and sprawl, and he
trails tangled in one stirrup helplessly.
Excuse my lack of self-control, these tears.
That cruel sight will haunt me all my years.
I saw him with my own eyes, sir, saw him towed
by the stallions he'd tamed himself and rode
in the cool of the morning, saw your son
dragged by the ponies he'd played polo on.
I hear him try to check them, *whoa there, whoa.*
It terrifies them more and still they go.
His body drags and twists, his clothes all tear.

[50]

He leaves a terrible trail of blood and hair.
That once fine handsome beauty with the look
of something dangling off a butcher's hook!
There was really nothing left to call a face.
At last the maddened horses slow their pace.
Staggering they slow down to a halt,
near where his princely forebears have their vault.
I follow, panting, sobbing. Sepoys wail.
Strewn flesh and bloodstains left an easy trail.
Rough rocks bearded with the boy's fine hair,
flesh on the sharp bamboo shoots! Everywhere!
Thomas, I say. He takes my hand. He tries
to open wide what once had been his eyes.
Dear friend, he gasps, *something has been sent*
to snatch my life away. I'm innocent.
When I am gone, look after her for me,
little Lilamani, lovingly.
Perhaps one day when father's disabused
and pities the dead son he once accused
beg him treat her kindly and restore . . .
With that his head fell back. He said no more.
The brave boy died, and left in my embrace
a lump of mangled flesh without a face.
Your 'gods' glut anger on the blameless one.
I doubt if you would recognize your son. *(Thunder)*

GOVERNOR Son, my son! All consolation in you gone.
I've murdered my own future. Thomas! Son!
India, you've served me all too well.
My life will be dragged out as one long hell.

(enter Memsahib unnoticed)

BURLEIGH Then Lilamani came, afraid of you,
and what your enmity would make you do.
She stares, gripped by some suffocating dream
at blood-red undergrowth and sickly steam.
She sees (what an object for a lover's eyes)
that mess that was her loved one and denies
the evidence before her, clings to doubt.

[51]

She sees the pile of flesh but looks about
and asks for him. How could she face that grim,
raw, featureless heap, and think it him?
At last she's certain and pours out her hate
on all the gods the Hindoos venerate,
then cold and moaning, sickened, almost dead
she crumples by the corpse she should have wed.
Relaying his last wish fulfills my vow.
My joy in life's all gone. I loathe it now.
It's blighted at the root. It's meaningless.
Your son is dead and *(indicating the Memsahib)*
                      there's his murderess!

GOVERNOR Good evening, Madam. Well, it seems you've won.
You've won your victory. I've lost my son.
Now new suspicions and misgivings start
sending tremors through my broken heart.
But what's the use? No, take your spoil. Enjoy
the harsh destruction of my gentle boy.
Relish it, and gloat. Go on, lick your lips.
The triumph (so far)'s all your Ladyship's.
I'm willingly blinkered. Don't want to know.
I'll think him a criminal if you say so.
There's been more than enough to make me weep
without my stirring up that murky deep.
Now I see it all. Given all my fame
so that the world can better see my shame.
This time there's no escape. No new disguise
will ever shield me from their staring eyes.
I want to cast off everything and run
from you, from India, my mangled son,
the very universe, and leave behind
the frontiers marked out for humankind.

MEMSAHIB No sir! Silence will no longer do!
Those accusations! They were all untrue.
He's innocent . . .

GOVERNOR   you were the very one
whose testimony made me curse my son.
You . . .!

[52]

MEMSAHIB   Richard! Listen! I need to reassure
          a father that his son died chaste and pure.
          The guilt was mine. For which I now atone.
          The inordinate desire was mine alone.
          The ayah took advantage of my state
          of shock and faintness to incriminate
          your son to you, and of her own accord
          accused him. She's had her just reward.
          Like her, I wanted instant suicide
          but wished to clear his name before I died.
          I wanted, needed to confess, and so
          I chose another, slower way to go —
(The Memsahib sinks to her knees)
          there's poison in my veins, and beat by beat
          the heart that once was blazing loses heat.
          It's all as if I saw you through dark gauze,
          through rain beginning like a slow applause.
          I hear it starting now, the rain, cool rain
          giving the blood-red earth new life again.
          Rain. Rain. Like purdah curtains. When I die
          the dawn will bring you all a clearer sky.
          / X / X / X / X / X
          / X / X / X / X / X
ADC She's dead!
GOVERNOR   But her black actions, they won't die.
          They'll blaze for ever in the memory.
          Clearer than day it all comes home to me.
          Now let me force myself to go and see
          what's left of him, and try to expiate
          my dabbling with strange gods I've come to hate.
          He must be buried with all honours due
          his mother's and my rank . . .
(enter Lilamani)
                              and as for you —
          Your family were mutineers. I realize
          I seem some savage brute to your young eyes.
          Your family mutinied. They raised the war.
          I had to administer the rule of law.

[53]

Your family, now mine, have borne the cost
of crossing certain bounds best left uncrossed.
Now try to ford, though times force us apart,
those frontiers of blood into my heart.

*As the Governor speaks the Chuprassie and servants kneel
and begin a chant which gradually becomes dominant. The
sound of rain like slow applause.*

Curtain